GW00691311

Convertible
Bond
Markets

Also by George A. Philips

JAPANESE WARRANT MARKETS
(with Kevin Connolly)

Convertible
Bond
Markets

George A. Philips

Foreword by Sajid Ramzan

© George A. Philips 1997
Foreword © Sajid Ramzan 1997

All rights reserved. No reproduction, copy or transmission
of this publication may be made without written permission.

No paragraph of this publication may be reproduced, copied
or transmitted save with written permission or in accordance
with the provisions of the Copyright, Designs and Patents
Act 1988, or under the terms of any licence permitting
limited copying issued by the Copyright Licensing Agency,
90 Tottenham Court Road, London W1P 9HE.

Any person who does any unauthorised act in relation to this
publication may be liable to criminal prosecution and civil
claims for damages.

The authors have asserted their rights to be identified as the
authors of this work in accordance with the Copyright,
Designs and Patents Act 1988.

First published 1997 by
MACMILLAN PRESS LTD
Houndmills, Basingstoke, Hampshire RG21 6XS
and London
Companies and representatives
throughout the world

ISBN 0-333-68749-3

A catalogue record for this book is available
from the British Library.

This book is printed on paper suitable for recycling and
made from fully managed and sustained forest sources.

10   9   8   7   6   5   4   3   2   1
06 05 04 03 02 01 00 99 98 97

Typeset in Great Britain by
Aarontype Limited,
Easton, Bristol

Printed and bound in Great Britain by
Antony Rowe Ltd,
Chippenham, Wiltshire

To my darling wife, Jacqueline
and my beautiful daughters, Christiana and Santina

Contents

List of Figures

List of Tables

Foreword

Over the last two decades, understanding of derivative products has increased at an incredible pace. It has not always been a painless learning experience, with well known catastrophes and crises marking the route. Nonetheless, derivatives of all kinds are now such an essential, fully integrated part of everybody's life that it is difficult to imagine the extent by which many businesses were constrained in the past. Convertible bonds are very particular kinds of derivatives which are most commonly issued by companies in lieu of equity or straight debt. The investor faces a promised cash flow and has the option of surrendering the bond for a preset number of shares in the underlying company.

In recent years, governments have utilised these securities as a means of privatising state interests, and blue chip multinational corporations have drawn on these hybrids to introduce flexibility into their capital structure. Moreover, companies based in the emerging markets have financed a considerable amount of their expansion plans by issuing convertible bonds. Within this context, originators of convertible bonds have been increasingly inventive and have introduced a number of very different structures so as to accommodate specific company requirements. Many large corporates have used converts as a way of reducing their crossholdings. In this case, there will be no dilution since the equity already exists.

As with all derivatives, the convertible bond market has matured considerably in recent years. The number of market neutral hedge funds exploiting pricing inefficiencies has been increasing. These managers may be categorised as those who arbitrage against stock and those who arbitrage against the credit of the issuer. The former group of investors attempt to extract value from mispricing of the equity by either buying the convertible and selling the underlying share if they think the option is cheap, or selling the bond short and buying the share in cases where they believe the option to be expensive. The other class of hedge manager is particularly interested in the straight bond or credit or the market's perception of the default risk for the issuer. The credit spread will vary over time depending on the market's perception of the 'well being' of the issuer. These managers might, for example, purchase the bond when the spread is wide and sell the risk free instrument, a government bond, in which case the convertible is cheap. When the spread narrows they will sell the convertible bond. It is now common practice for convertible bonds to be asset swapped. This entails taking a convert, composed of a straight bond and option, and stripping the bond of its component parts. This achieves two synthetic instruments, a synthetic bond and a warrant. For some of the most powerful investment banks this has provided an extremely profitable means of exploiting inherent value in these securities.

Not surprisingly, a significant proportion of outright equity fund managers on the whole are still not really in touch with convertible securities. There are many instances where certain inefficiencies cannot be exploited by arbitrageurs and yet the largest holders of the same underlying equity may completely ignore the instruments. Advantages of incremental yield, estimable downside protection, increased liquidity and very good equity participation are all too easily tossed aside. Fund managers might argue, 'I don't buy a stock that I think will go down!' or 'In theory they might be great, but convertibles don't move like you want in practice!'.

The author of *Convertible Bond Markets* is a partner at the global emerging market investment bank, Caspian Securities, where he is the Head of Convertible Bonds and Warrants. George has a full understanding of convertible bond instruments. His breadth of experience as a salesman, proprietary trader, hedger and fund manager are exhibited in this book which covers some difficult subjects but in a practical manner. Convertibles are difficult to value from an academic standpoint, yet the book leads to reader through the field with a need for only basic mathematics. Over the past twelve years, George has sought to exploit anomalies in corporate derivative pricing and was one of the first investors to hedge baskets of warrants with index futures.

SAJID RAMZAN
Deutsche Bank Arbitrage Department

Preface

This book has been written to fill a gap in the study of corporate derivatives. In all books on convertible bonds there is not, in many ways, a complete pricing model presented. Debate continues over something as basic as the underlying asset to be considered, or whether it makes sense to assume constant interest rates. The convertible bond market has gained increasing significance on a global basis with particularly notable growth among very fast-growing companies, hungry for capital. Many such companies are not even rated by major credit rating agencies as yet, despite investor appeal. As a result, obvious questions such as credit spreads are often conveniently pushed aside.

The theory and analysis presented throughout is not intended to be market specific on the one hand, or time dependent on the other: there is no reason for any of the arguments to date. For this reason, market or institutional peculiarities are largely ignored. This kind of information is easily obtainable from brokers or periodicals, and although important should be couched within a general theory of convertible bonds. One certainly needs to know what kinds of questions to ask. For example, is it possible to short the underlying share in the country under consideration? Are there restrictions on foreign ownership? Are prices 'clean' or 'dirty'? Is withholding tax charged? And so on.

The book is designed to teach those who really want to learn about convertible bonds. The mathematics is not very demanding, but parts of the book will require re-reading. The study should provide sound training for brokers and fund managers of all kinds, whether hedge, outright equity investors, fixed income, or otherwise. The book will also help in the process of risk management by those making markets.

Chapter 1 focuses on the establishment of minimum arbitrage boundaries for convertible bonds, as well as providing a setting for these derivative instruments. Chapter 2 considers convertible financing options on the part of the company. Chapters 3 and 4 are of crucial importance and will enable investors and academics to arrive at a fair price for converts. This is one of the most important, if not *the* most important, question to be asked of the market. No matter what your persuasion, you will want to know whether the instrument is cheap or not. This chapter also illustrates various sensitivity ratios.

Chapters 5 and 6 relate to interest rate and credit adjusted spreads respectively. Both these subjects are usually largely overlooked in books on the subject. An overview of both subject matters are provided, as well as how practically to deal with the issues and risks involved. Interest rate hedging, default premium and assessing the floor on a bond are just some of the topics of study.

Chapter 7 looks at the subject of being 'long volatility'. This chapter studies problems in pricing bonds in practice, as well as elaborating on many of the assumptions underpinning the model. It then goes on to show the process of hedging 'long volatility'. Importantly, there is an emphasis on the nature of the profit profile of such a strategy by accounting for and understanding actual returns which differ from expected returns. Unlike exchange traded option markets, there have been occasions when corporate derivatives have traded at substantial discounts to their theoretical values for sustained periods of time. In fact, they have often become even cheaper. These types of issues are rarely discussed in financial literature.

Chapter 8 goes on to introduce aspects of multivariate hedging. Little has been written on the use of futures to offset equity risk, as opposed to using individual short stock positions. Many preconceived views of tracking error and hedge adjustments, for example, are reconsidered.

It is hoped that this book will encourage an appreciation and further understanding of convertibles and will be of practical use by new entrants to the market place, salespeople, traders, administrative staff, stock loan staff, or custodians.

Since 1985, I have been a research analyst, salesman, proprietary trader and Fund manager. Given my day-to-day involvement in the financial markets, it has often been questioned whether it actually makes sense to detail strategies or further an understanding of the field by writing on the subject. Markets are very dynamic and individuals will always be advancing theories to exploit prevailing opportunities. I have taken a lot of time focusing attention on what I believe to be core areas of interest and controversy. My wife, Jacqueline Stewart Philips, inspired me to write *Convertible Bond Markets* and was unfailing in her encouragement. It is difficult to express my gratitude to David Rogers and David Philips who provided extensive personal and technical support throughout. Dr Kevin Connolly has always proved to be someone I can learn from in the field of derivatives. A number of individuals made very helpful suggestions or have been a pleasure to work with over the years. In particular, I thank Sajid Ramzan, Daniel Wood, John Lowrey, Russell Pfeiffer, Sleem Hassan, Simon Haynes-Oliver, Justin Donegan and Shahid Ramzan.

Finally, I owe a debt of gratitude to everyone at Caspian, the global emerging markets group, who have opened my eyes to the profitable specialist opportunities that prevail outside the Euromarket.

GEORGE A. PHILIPS

1: Convertible Bonds

INTRODUCTION

The field of 'derivatives' encompasses very different financial securities which all derive their existence from some primary or underlying security including equities, all types of indices, and commodities. There are even pollution futures. Many of these so-called 'derivatives' have similar characteristics, but it is quite common for experts in one specific field to have little or no knowledge at all of another area. Derivatives have a long and illustrious history, but in recent years exponential growth has brought many problems with it. Financial crises centred on declared bankruptcies in Barings Bank, Metallgesellschaft, Orange County and massive losses at Sumitomo Corporation are just a few examples where billions of dollars have been lost due to a mixture of misunderstanding, abuse and poor risk management. Although a considerable amount of the analysis and theory presented throughout this book may be applied much more widely, almost all attention will be focused on particular derivatives known as convertible bonds, converts, or CBs.

A convertible security is a bond or preferred stock issued by a company which gives the right but not the obligation to convert into another security, most commonly the company's underlying shares.

Converts are *hybrid* instruments – they display both equity and debt characteristics. Common stock or share equity represents ownership in an enterprise, usually providing for dividends and voting rights. In contrast to an equity, a bond represents outstanding debt of a given enterprise, and will usually promise to pay a fixed principal on a stipulated date, with interest payments over its life.

There are quite a number of different types of convertible securities that will be seen throughout the book. In contrast to the convertible bond so far defined, *convertible preferred stock* is stock convertible into a fixed ratio of common shares. Another common type is the so-called *exchangeable convertible bond*, which entitles holders to convert into shares of another company.

Converts are special in the sense that option components are *'embedded'* within the overall security. This has presented analysts with considerable problems over the years in the appraisal of these instruments.

The aim of this chapter is not simply to define and list concepts such as 'parity', 'bond value' or 'investment floor' and the like, but specifically to lay sound fundamentals for pricing convertible bond securities. In some ways, this may disappoint a group of readers. The institutional infrastructure and history of particular market places are largely ignored, because specific information of this kind is constantly changing and included in all kinds of brokerage reports printed weekly or monthly. The idea is in fact to provide a general framework for considering convertibles. For this reason, we first explore the process of issuance and fixing of terms. We are then in a good position to succinctly outline concepts of parity, investment value and minimum arbitrage boundaries. Finally, background to the global convertible bond markets is considered.

TERMS AND CONDITIONS

Let us assume that an Indian corporation wishes to raise the equivalent of Rupees 3.4 billion in order to be able expand its production capabilities in Asia. It might be able to do this in a number of ways. An investment bank will typically advise the borrower on which means of financing is optimal. The company's existing capital structure will be examined among other factors to determine the currency, maturity of the new issue as well as future demands.

If India Corp. borrows US$100 million in the form of a regular *straight bond*, as opposed to a convertible bond, the issue might be priced in the way shown in Table 1.1.

Despite a need for it, there is usually very little bond market terminology or bond mathematics in convertible bond literature. Furthermore, many readers

Table 1.1: Straight bond, terms and conditions

Coupon	:	8.5% (semi-annual)
Maturity	:	1 May 2003
Issue size	:	US$100,000,000
Denomination	:	US$5,000
Number of bonds	:	20,000
Issue price	:	100 % or 'par'
Lead manager	:	Leading investment bank

will be more equity orientated and left pondering the significance of points raised. We will slowly introduce bond concepts.

On the day of issue in our example, seven year US$ government debt is yielding 6.5%. At the time of issue, this security is yielding 8.5% and is said to be yielding 200 basis points 'over the curve'. (A basis point is one hundredth of 1% or 0.01%.) Most readers will be familiar with the concept that more credit worthy companies tend to be able to borrow at more favourable rates than less credit worthy companies. This particular company is assumed to have a very good credit rating. Other less reputable companies may have to borrow at higher rates, with their bonds therefore yielding, say, 250 or 300 basis points over a given benchmark yield. This will suffice for the present but reasons for this will be discussed at length later in the book.

The length of the loan is seven years and each bond is issued at 100% of US$5,000. It is standard practice for bond prices to be quoted as a percentage of the nominal, principal or par value. If the price in the market place fell to 98%, each bond held by an investor would have fallen in value to US$4,900 (i.e. 0.98×5000). It should be apparent that the total number of bonds outstanding in this particular issue is calculated as the amount borrowed divided by the denomination of each bond (i.e. $100,000,000/5,000 = 20,000$). If we buy one million 'nominal' at a price of 98%, it means that we buy 200 bonds (i.e. $1000,000/5,000$) for a total outlay of US$980,000, not US$1,000,000.

The company has borrowed US$100 million. In seven years' time, this bond will redeem at par – the company will repay the loan, or will be forced to default if it fails to meet its coupon or redemption obligations. In the meantime, the company is obliged to pay coupons of 8.5% of US$5,000 to bond-holders on a semi-annual basis (i.e. US$212.5 every six months per bond or a total of US$4,250,000 to all bond-holders). Sometimes a convertible bond may be redeemed at an amount that is different from the principal value of the bond. Such bonds are said to be premium redemption and bonds with put options. This is particularly common among many convertibles issued by French companies. The frequency of coupon payments differs from issue to issue.

The lead manager is responsible for winning the mandate from the borrower to bring the issue to the market, organising the distribution of the new deal as well as co-ordinating efforts. Co-managers will be selected and final terms will have been arrived at in consultation with the borrower. There is often a long standing relationship between the borrower and 'lead', but the market has become highly lucrative and competitive. Lead managers have become increasingly innovative in their recommendations to companies in terms of the different kinds of structured deals that may be finalised.

We are now in a better position to consider the terms and conditions of a standard convertible bond issue which has no 'bells and whistles' attached. The issuing company is still India Corp.

3

Table 1.2: Plain vanilla CB, terms and conditions

Coupon	:	3.50 % (semi-annual)
Maturity	:	1 May 2003
Issue size	:	US$100,000,000
Denomination	:	US$5,000
Number of bonds	:	20,000
Issue price	:	100 %
Conversion price	:	Rs 100
Shares/bond	:	1700
Fixed FX	:	Rs 34 = US$1
Parity	:	87 %
Premium	:	15%
Investment value	:	74.5 %
Market price	:	103.25–104.25

We are no longer considering a security which is just fixed income or debt. In this example of a convertible issue, India Corp. has issued a bond which gives the right but not the obligation to convert into the underlying shares of the company at a prespecified price, referred to as the conversion, strike or exercise price, over the next seven years (see Table 1.2). The conversion right or option of this particular issue *may or may not* be taken up at any time over the life of the bond and is referred in the market place as being an '*American*' option as opposed to a '*European*' option, the latter only providing for conversion at the end of the bond's life. Almost all convertible bonds tend to be 'American style'.

Let's first consider the option component of this particular security. For sake of simplicity, the share price in this example is assumed to be Rs 87 at the time terms are fixed. The conversion price in this case is set approximately 15% above the prevailing share price, i.e. Rs 100. Such a bond would be said to have been issued on a 15% conversion premium. In reality, the conversion price may as easily be set say 0%, 5% or 20% above the share price. The structure or type of convertible bond will be determined by the company's preferences and potential investor demands. We will consider how bonds with different coupons and premiums may come to the market when we focus on the borrower's perspective in Chapter 2, but let's stay with the present example for the moment.

Each US$5000 denominated bond converts into 1700 shares per bond, also referred to as the conversion ratio. If the underlying equity and the denomination of the bond were in the same currency (i.e. Rupees), then the formula for calculating the ratio would be:

Conversion ratio = Bond denomination/Conversion price   (1.1)

This is obviously not the case in our example. Our company is borrowing in US$ when the bond converts into Rupees. The convertible will be structured such that in the event of conversion, the proceeds total the same irrespective of the movements in the foreign exchange rate:

Conversion ratio = (Bond denomination × Fixed FX)/Conversion price (1.2)

Many bonds may be denominated in one currency but convertible into the currency of the underlying shares. For example, the funds may have been raised in US$ but the bond converts into Hong Kong Dollars or Thai Bahts. In this case, the conversion ratio is simply found by first multiplying the bond denomination in (1.1) by the official currency figure taken in the indenture at the time of fixing, known as the 'fixed' exchange rate.

The legal obligations of issuers and rights of bondholders are contained in the *indenture* of the bond. All the relevant terms, conditions and obligations are outlined in the *prospectus* or offering memorandum and provided by the lead manager at the beginning of the subscription period in a preliminary form, known as the 'red herring'.

PARITY

We are now in a position to view the share component of the convertible bond. The term *parity* or *intrinsic value* is often used with regard to convertible bonds to describe the value of the underlying share price, expressed as a percentage of the face value of the bond in the home currency. Once again, if the bond and underlying equity are denominated in the same currency, parity may be calculated as follows:

Parity = Share price/Conversion price (1.3)

or   = Share price × Conversion ratio

**   = 87%**

If there is a foreign exchange issue, parity is calculated as follows:

$$\textbf{Parity*} = \frac{\textbf{(Share price × Conversion ratio)}}{\textbf{Bond principal in currency of equity}} \quad (1.4)$$

Under this scenario, the company raises capital at a cost of 3.5% p.a. compared with straight debt of 8.5%. This is because the company is giving up something of considerable value. The company has given the CB investor the right to convert into the underlying shares, which would result in equity being diluted by US$100 million (see Figure 1.1).

It is quite straightforward to see that the intrinsic or parity line graphed in Figure 1.1 is the profile of the underlying share. It may be incredibly obvious, but it is important to spell out the fact that it is a 45 degree line or that the

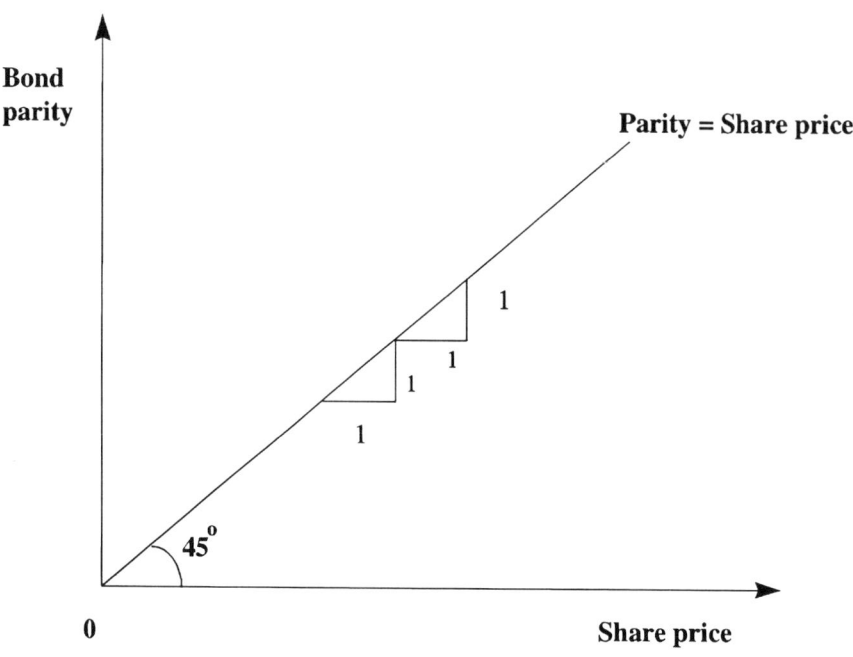

Figure 1.1: Intrinsic value of a convertible bond

gradient of this line is 1. If the share price increases/decreases by Rs 10, the parity of the bond increases/decreases by Rs 10. This parity boundary is crucial since it is essentially *one of the minimum arbitrage boundaries.* If the convertible falls to a discount to parity, it would be possible to buy the bond and simultaneously sell the underlying stock short, thus effectively locking in an arbitrage profit.

In practice, the actual arbitrage boundary would be net parity – allowing for transactions costs, and the fact that if the bonds are converted, the investor gives up any accrued interest. Furthermore, effectively selling short may be costly or not possible due to lack of available 'borrowing lines' for the underlying share concerned.

INVESTMENT VALUE OR 'FLOOR'

Now, returning our attention to Table 1.2, let's ask ourselves what the price is of a seven year straight bond, paying 3.5% semi-annual coupons and trading 200 basis points over the government yield of 6.5%. Assuming all other things equal, the answer is that investors would be prepared to pay 74.5% for such a

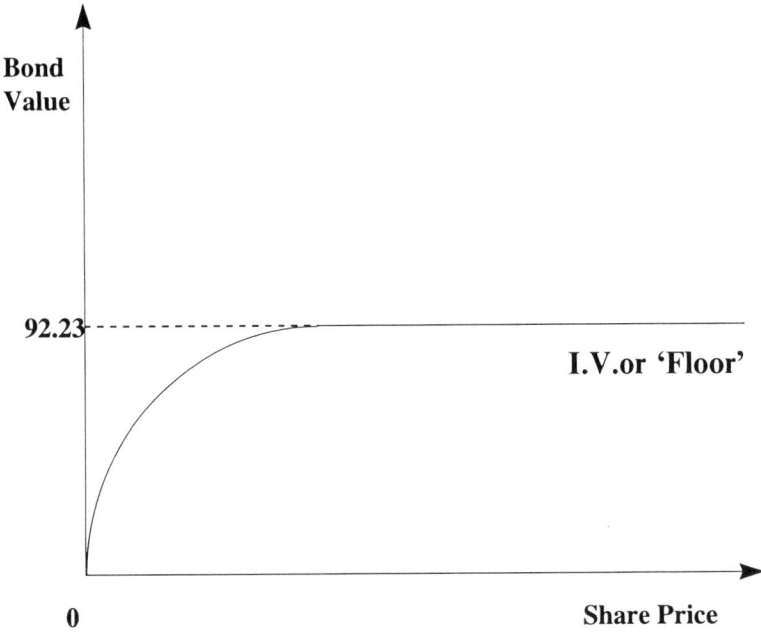

Figure 1.2: Investment value of a convertible bond

straight bond because this is the price at which the yield would equate to 8.5% (see Figure 1.2). We will show how to calculate such bond values shortly.

So in the case of our convertible, even without conversion features, the security would be worth 74.5%. If this hypothetical straight bond yielded more than 8.50% – say, 120 basis points over the curve – investors could switch from other fixed income with the same rating and characteristics, until no differential existed. This is essentially the *second minimum arbitrage boundary* and is referred to as the *investment value* (IV) or '*floor*' of the bond.

The investment value is drawn naively in Figure 1.2. Although it may appear common sense that the investment floor tails off at an increasing pace to zero as the share price falls to very low share prices, it is a subject not often addressed in literature. In reality, the nature of the curve becomes erratic when future promised payments come into question. Some of the readers will be familiar with practical examples of bonds whose floor has fallen away in this fashion during periods of crisis and concern over whether a company will remain solvent in the near future. e.g. *Polly Peck 7.25 % (1/4/2005)*, or *Fokker 4.75% (15/11/1999)*. At very low share prices where solvency may be in question or where companies may be considered as being in default, bonds are sometimes referred to as '*junk*'. This whole area will be analysed in Chapter 6, but should nevertheless be noted already. However, it is worth noting at this point that just because the share price of a convertible bond may be very low relative to the conversion price (e.g. parity may be 10% or 15%), it does not necessarily mean that the company's ability to repay debt will be in question.

Except for that part of the 'floor' where solvency is in question, the price of the bond is independent of share price moves. Again, it may be stating the obvious, but the gradient of the line is zero. That is, for every Rs 10 move in the underlying share, the bond price remains unchanged. It is important to be aware of this point even at this stage.

We are now in a position to overlay these arbitrage boundaries as shown in Figure 1.3. Many interesting points begin to reveal themselves. If the share price or parity was so low that the bondholders' option to convert into the underlying was completely worthless, the convert would trade at its bond floor. Similarly, at this stage we will say that if the share price was so high that any bond floor sitting below it provided little downside protection, and yields were identical, then the bond would trade at parity. However, in between these points, the hybrid nature of the instrument deserves an option value. A good deal of the book will be concerned with the evaluation and understanding of the price at which the convert should be trading.

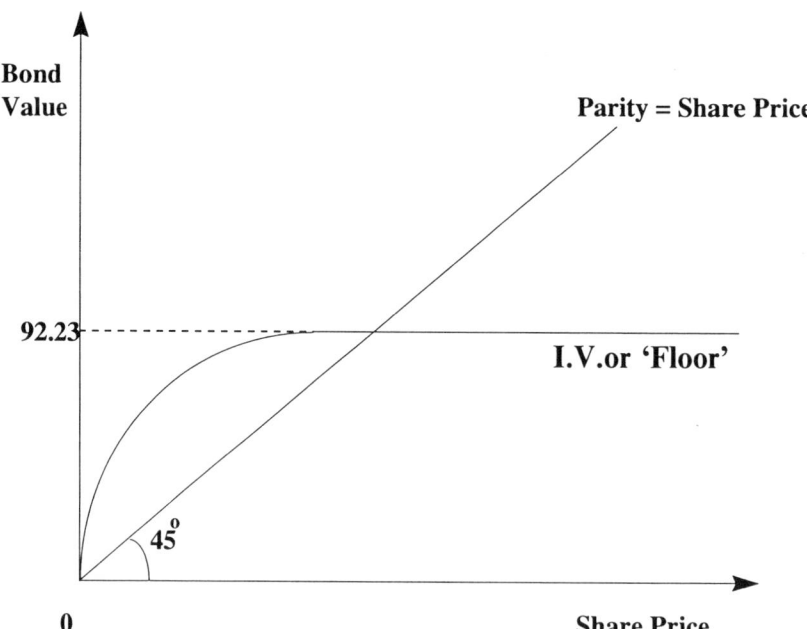

Figure 1.3: Convertible bond minimum price boundaries

We will continue by first looking at basic terms and conditions of the issue. From Table 1.2, we can see that the convert is actually trading 103.25 bid–104.25 offered.

If an investor is prepared to pay 104.25 (US$5212.5) for the bond, he is effectively paying 17.25 points more for the bond than he would for shares that it converts into. He is said to be paying 17.25 points *premium*. Alternatively this is most often expressed as a percentage and calculated as follows:

Premium = (Market price of convert/Parity) – 1

$$= (104.25/87) - 1 = 19.83\% \tag{1.5}$$

This is shown diagrammatically as in Figure 1.4.

Particularly because it is so easy to calculate, premium has been misused considerably. It means literally what it says – 'how much of a premium one is paying to hold the convert as opposed to holding the underlying equity'. It is not in itself a measure of expensiveness or cheapness. We cannot say, for example, that a convert with a 1% premium offers better value than a convert which is carrying a 10% premium: it may be the case that given the option which the '10% premium bond' provides, it should merit paying what amounts to 20% premium.

Let's consider why premium expands and contracts and furthermore, what factors different kinds of investors should identify.

Consider Figure 1.5. The shaded area above the parity line is a graphical representation of premium. Basic features need to be understood. At high share prices, such as that represented by '*A*', the parity of the bond exceeds the floor by such a great margin that almost no benefit is to be gained by the bond floor feature For this reason, the convertible bond will mimic the underlying stock – it *synthesises equity*. At this share price level, the extent by which the bond

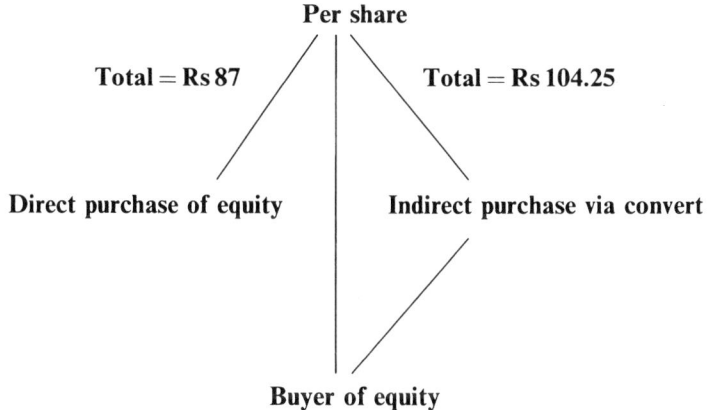

Figure 1.4: Paying a premium

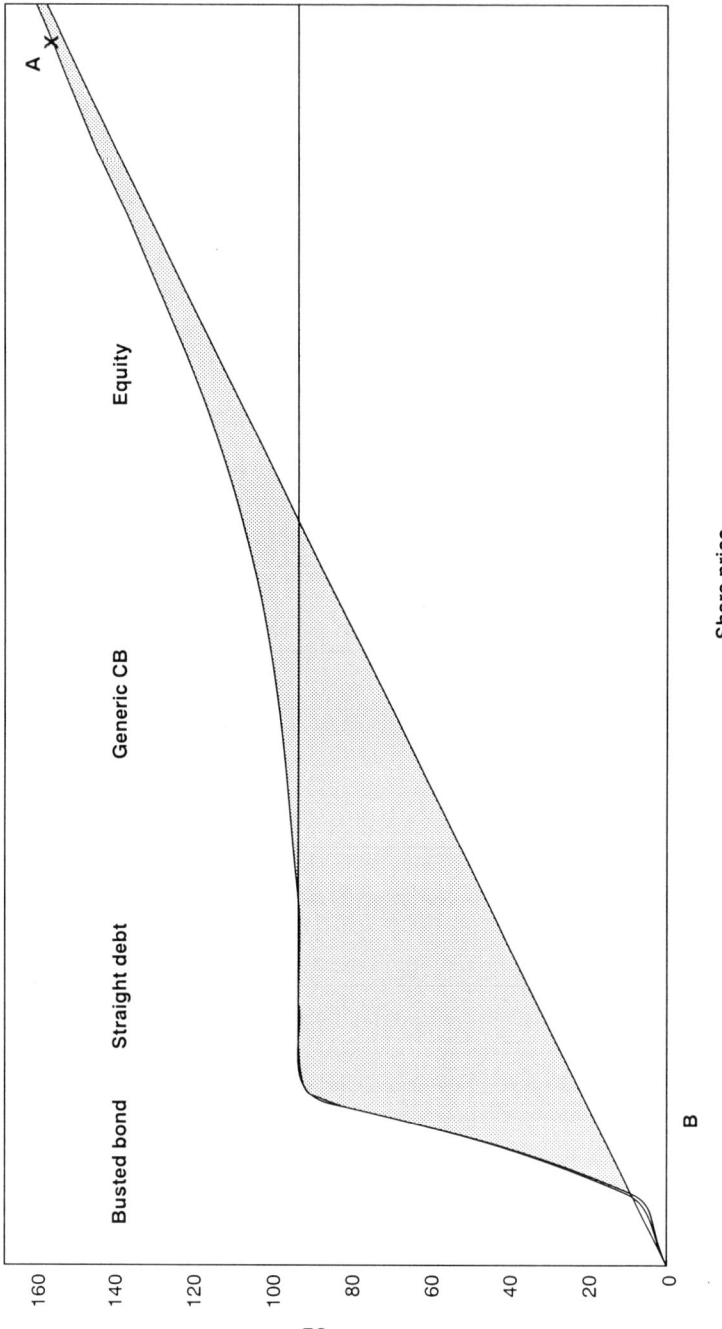

Figure 1.5: Graphical representation of premium

should trade above or below parity is explained by the yield advantage or disadvantage that the bond offers over the stock.

The current yield of a convertible bond is the coupon payment on the bond expressed as a percentage of its market price. If the coupon is 3.5%, as in our example, and the market price is 104.25, the current yield is approximately 3.36% p.a:

Current yield = Coupon/Market price of CB (1.6)

If the current yield exceeds the dividend yield on the underlying share, the bond is said to have a *yield advantage*. In this case if the share has a yield of 0.5%, then the CB has a yield advantage of 2.86%:

Yield advantage = Current yield − Dividend yield (1.7)

Equity investors find the concept of 'break-even' appealing. That is, how many years it takes for the premium on the bond to be recouped by the current yield advantage. Simple break-even may be calculated as follows:

Break-even = (Bond price − Parity)/Yield advantage (1.8)

Ideal for investors with an equity mandate are those convertibles which capture considerable equity participation on share price increases, but which very quickly behave less and less like equity on share price decreases. Equity investors should be aware of situations where bonds provide for this combination of favourable characteristics. A common mistake has been for investors to look for the price of the bond to tell them when the CB is likely to move into the 'hybrid' territory shown in Figure 1.5. This is false.

Let us introduce a simple but extremely effective concept. Of particular interest in Figure 1.5 is the ratio of parity of the bond to the investment value. This ratio will be referred to as S/IV. When the parity of the bond has moved far above the bond floor (e.g. $S/IV = 1.75$), the downside protection offered by the bond becomes less and less meaningful. Therefore, as already shown, the bond will trade more and more like equity. When the share price falls to low levels (e.g. $S/IV = 0.35$ or point 'B' in Figure 1.5), the share needs to appreciate so dramatically before maturity in order for the option to be worth anything that the bond will trade like straight debt.

THE GLOBAL CONVERTIBLE BOND MARKET

Cox *et al.* (1985) use various criteria to assess the performance and maturity of the options markets:

1   **Size and profitability**
2   **Liquidity**
3   **Transactions speed**
4   **Fairness**
5   **Effects on other markets**

Convertible bonds were first issued in the USA, over one hundred years ago by railroad companies, and companies which needed to tap a larger array of investor types. Particularly high growth has been witnessed out of the 'Tigers' of the Pacific Rim in recent years. It is pointless to put too much emphasis on estimates of the size of the global convertible bond market at present, since the environment is very dynamic, with constant new issuance and conversion taking place.

It is interesting just to see the relative importance of the market at the time of writing. It has been estimated that the global convertible bond market has a market capitalisation of US$360 billion, excluding all domestic markets except for the USA and Japan. By far the largest issuance is from Japan and the USA. In many respects, the needs of a number of the companies in emerging markets now are not totally dissimilar to their forebears in America. The estimate would further increase dramatically if we were to include the issuance of 'cum' warrant bonds (i.e. Warrants plus 'ex' bonds), which are essentially convertible bonds.

In order to be able to assess the breadth of a particular securities market, as well as understanding it, it is useful to be aware of the different kinds of investors involved, their risk persuasion, and how they interact. One way to look at investments is in terms of 'expected returns $(E(R))$ and risk (σ) space', as shown in Figure 1.6.

A *rational investor* will select one investment over another if for the same level of risk, the former investment offers a higher expected return. In such circumstances, we say that the former investment *dominates* the latter and lies 'Northwest' of the frontier above. Risk free debt is first plotted above for a given expected return. Sovereign or corporate debt which has risk, requires a higher expected return and outright exposure to convertible securities lies somewhere between fixed income and equity in this risk/return space. A reason why convertibles appeal to so many investors of differing persuasions is that they will shift investors 'Northwest' in risk/return space if they are underpriced.

It is possible to use derivatives to *synthesise* many or all of the return characteristics of these different investments. This is the major reason for almost exponential growth in this field over the last three decades. For example, in perfect markets, those long of converts versus a given short

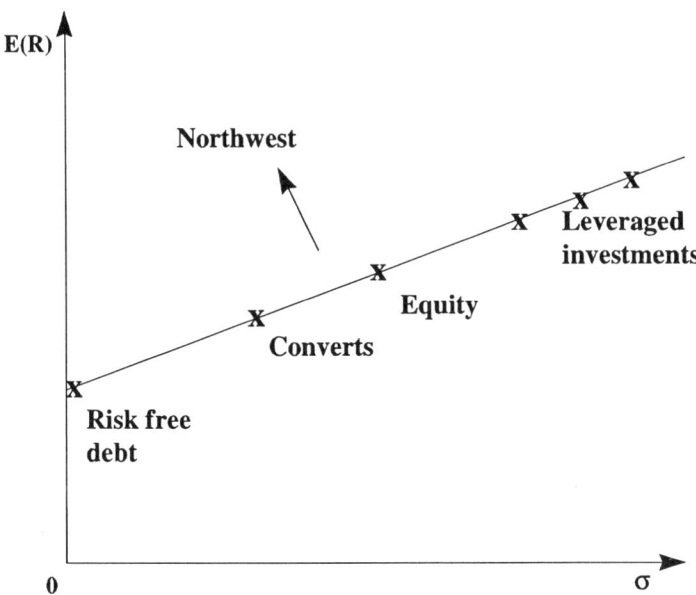

Figure 1.6: Expected returns and risk

position in the underlying stock are synthesising fixed income. Many investment groups have an objective to shift returns 'Northwest' of this 'efficient frontier', and in so doing increase expected returns for any given level of risk.

The reason that this framework is particularly useful when considering converts is that the investor may only be using the derivative because it is 'undervalued' and may be taken alone or in combination with other securities to synthesise an enhanced position. To see in practice what this means, let's look at a 'spectrum of investors' in Figure 1.7. The interaction of all these investors goes to make up the market place for convertible securities globally.

For more risk averse investors, let's first think of fixed income investors. As already seen from our analysis of minimum arbitrage boundaries, when the share price is considerably below the conversion price of the bond, the option portion of the security may be afforded little or no value at all. Such fixed income investors may be responsible for corporate bond investments in a given region or a particular country and will typically consider the convertible bond if the yield on the security is greater than or equal to that of a comparable straight.

There is a community which is arbitrage or hedge orientated, in one form or another. In examples of classic 'long convert short equity' trades which are dynamically adjusted, the return profile synthesised is that of fixed income, if

13

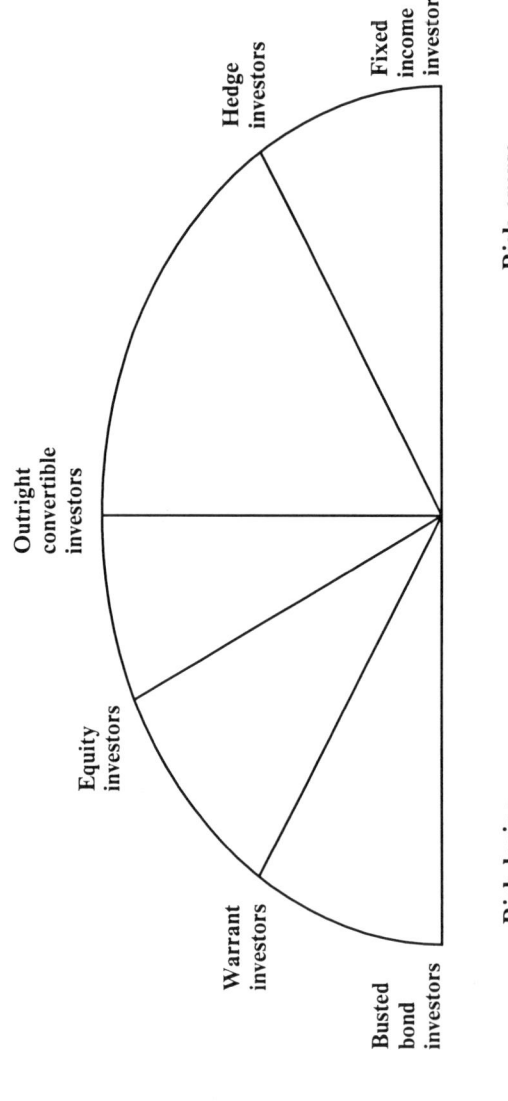

Figure 1.7: Risk spectrum

the instruments were fairly valued. This particular investment stance forms the basis of Chapter 7 – 'Long Volatility'. In option theory, this is also the main building block for fair pricing. Understanding the function of different market participants is crucial. For example, any region where it is very difficult or extremely expensive to borrow shares will typically result in market inefficiencies from which other investors should be able to benefit.

Of course, converts may be used on an outright basis, for the sake of themselves by those looking for these particular return characteristics. There are many funds globally which are termed 'convertible funds' which do exactly this.

By definition, if convertibles are used by hedge funds to synthesise fixed income, the 'mirror image' is to synthesise equity. Instead of shorting the underlying equity, the investor will simply sell the shares on position and buy a given proportion of converts. Alternatively, if the investor wishes to gain initial exposure to the equity he may buy a given proportion of the bonds to start with.

If it were possible to 'swap' out the fixed income portion of a convertible bond, then we would simply be long of a warrant. This is exactly what is done by many investors. For example, some of the hedgers already mentioned swap out the fixed income portion of the convert and then trade what is effectively a warrant position against the underlying security. Given the nature of this trade, a minimum size is often a constraint to begin with.

The final category noted on the 'risk spectrum' graph in Figure 1.7 is that of so-called 'busted bond' investors. 'Busted bond' refers to bonds of speculative rather than investment grade. These 'fallen angels' may trade at very high yields, reflecting investor perception of the borrower's ability to meet promised coupon and redemption payments. A number of well known financial institutions invest in such distressed securities if they believe that the market has misinterpreted the company's ability to meet promised payments. One example to consider would be that of Banco de Galicia in 1995. As with many other companies at the time, economic crisis in Latin America drove equities lower and with it trading distress widened the CB theoretical spread so that it yielded 2500 basis points over the curve. All of these investment strategies will be investigated in greater depth throughout the remainder of the book.

Unlike options markets, terms and conditions, pricing and market structures for corporate derivatives are not normalised. Some bonds trade 'dirty' while others trade 'clean' (i.e. the bonds trade with or without accrued interest already in the price). Some bonds may be issued on a 2.5% premium, while others may be issued on a 22.5% premium. In fact many convertibles are issued with differing complicated and 'wordy' embedded options and clauses. This makes it very important that any 'small print' in the indenture is read carefully. Some market participants have benefited tremendously by employing analysts which specialise in this specific task. Such conditions allow for poor transmission of information at times and therefore more inefficient pricing of convertibles. Inefficiencies certainly make for more interesting and obviously more profitable markets. This is a suitable place to answer an often asked question: 'If investor A buys a cheap newly issued convert, surely someone must be losing out?' This is indeed true. If a convertible is issued too cheaply, shareholders in the underlying equity are the losers. Regulation and exchange listing are not necessarily the answer, however. There are many benefits which come from a looser market framework, including increased liquidity in many cases.

In particular, the Eurobond market has become increasingly important for newly issued convertible bonds. This is, to a large extent, an 'acknowledgement of the global equity and debt market'. This falls under the aegis of the International Securities Market Association (ISMA), approved as an international securities self-regulatory organisation. The objectives of ISMA are:

- To implement and enforce rules governing the orderly functioning of the market
- To encourage improvements in international capital markets and to provide services and assistance to participants
- To enhance relations between its members and with related national and international markets.

Many of the 'over the counter' (OTC) convertible bond markets are often found to be more liquid than those that are traded on exchanges, despite objections of 'lack of transparency' in the market. It might be further argued that tighter bid/offer spreads are exhibited on exchanges, but once again, it is merely a question of understanding the benefits which come from the products being traded OTC, and that the OTC 'touch' may in fact be tighter in many cases, depending from issue to issue on factors such as individual liquidity. If commissions or transactions costs are to be considered with that of the underlying equity, for sake of comparing apples with apples, we should normalise the procedure by estimating costs on a per share basis to gain the same equity exposure – convertibles generally compare very favourably.

One should also think of the question of liquidity in a relative sense to that of the underlying equity. Outright equity investors, particularly in smaller listed or OTC companies, can increase liquidity in very 'thin' volume stocks. In this respect, convertibles remain very much under-utilised globally. In a number of emerging markets where there are foreign investor limits, convertible bond issues certainly enhance liquidity. This often has important implications. For example, it has not been unusual for foreign investors to pay 30–40% premiums for given Global Depository Receipts (GDRs) because of a lack of availability of local shares. Equity investors should be very aware of

CBs issued on such companies either exercisable into the local share or the GDR. Finally, as regards the impact and effects on other markets, we will address this question in Chapter 7 in the context of dilution.

2: Convertible Financing

There are a number of convertible variants that an issuer may consider. Most simply, we may think of these ranging from being tantamount to equity at one extreme or debt at the other. Another way of viewing the situation is to think of the probability of dilution. In this chapter, we consider different types of bonds that the borrower may issue.

There are many reasons why companies are said to issue convertible bonds. Figure 2.1 is a spectrum of some of the different kinds of convertible bonds that might be issued by companies, ranging from structures which closely resemble straight debt throught to bonds which are really tantamount to equity. This ability to structure tailor made financial instruments to suit the borrower is one of the important reasons why many companies prefer to issue convertible bonds at times rather than straight debt or equity equivalents. Throughout the spectrum, dilution is certainly postponed until some future date at least, although the probability of it occurring varies. The point is that companies are keen to at least postpone diluting earnings per share, but for some this may be a more imminent concern.

Some points which are common to convertibles of all kinds include not only a globalisation of the investor base, but just as importantly a broadening of the nature of these investors. (Different investor participation in convertibles formed part of Chapter 1.) International name recognition among debt, equity, outright convertible funds and arbitrage type investors may be crucial for a company's future fund raising efforts. This is more apparent where companies' expansion plans may be stifled by domestic regulatory constraints.

Convertibles provide for flexibility within the capital structure, and may play the part of foreign exchange management. It should be clear, however, that the audience for companies which issue convertible bonds is diverse in itself. At one extreme, convertibles have been issued in industrialised economies by governments eager to privatise state interests and multinational 'blue chip' corporations, and at the other extreme they have provided smaller companies with the opportunity to aggressively raise finance. An extreme example of the latter has been a more recent trend for very low capitalised companies (most notably biotechnology orientated) to raise funds through private placements almost overnight (i.e. Reg. 'S' deals).

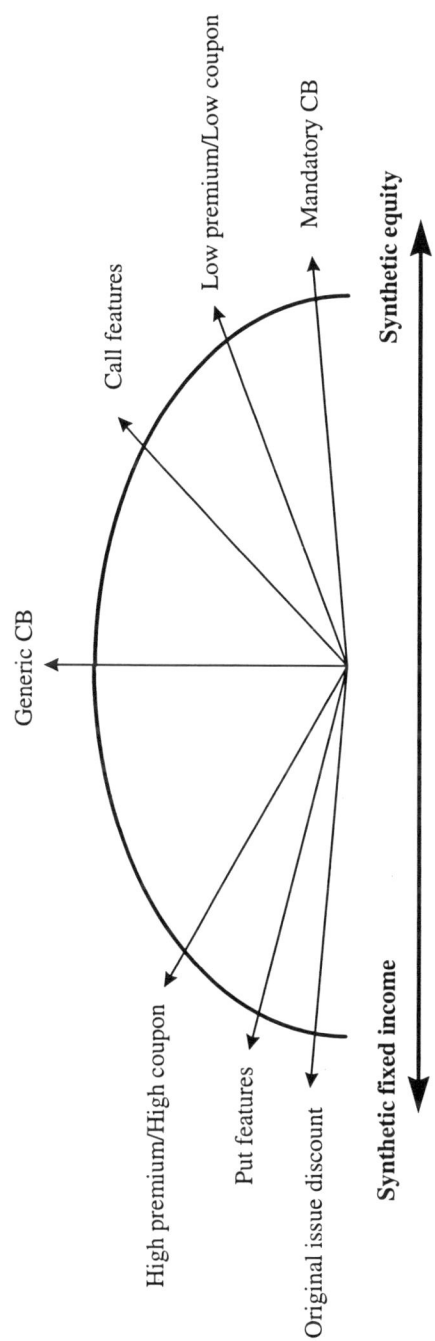

Figure 2.1: Spectrum of convertible bond issues

Within the context of a plain vanilla CB we also see how the interest burden is actually reduced. The trade off, of course, is that equity is likely to be diluted at some point (see Figure 2.2).

GENERIC CONVERTIBLE BOND

We first consider an issuer that wants to raise US$100 million, with repayment of the loan scheduled for five years. Let's say that US$ 5 year government debt yields 6.96% and our company needs to pay 9.96% to attract investors. In order for straight debt with a coupon of 5% (annual) and five year life to yield 9.96%, investors would only be prepared to pay 80.87%. As explained, this straight bond equivalent value is also referred to as investment value or the 'floor' of the bond. In the example, the company could alternatively sell the bond for 100% if it provides an embedded option to convert into the underlying shares over the next five years.

The interest burden has been reduced from US$9,960,000 p.a. to US$5,000,000 p.a. If none of the bonds are converted into equity over the life of the instrument, the company would have raised capital very cheaply. However, if the bonds are converted, in addition to the coupon burden, the shareholders' equity will be *diluted* by US$100,000,000.

In Figure 2.2, the five year CB with a 5% coupon has been issued on a 17% premium (i.e. the conversion price is 17% above the prevailing share price). On share price increases, the bond does not move 'one for one' with the equity at first. Neither does the security resemble straight debt – it yields 496 basis points under a comparable straight. Moreover, unlike a straight bond there is a certain response to share price increases/decreases. This is a plain vanilla convertible bond which really behaves like a hybrid of equity and debt. There are no embedded call or put provisions in the security. At new issue, the bond has a floor of 80.87 % or equivalently almost 20 points downside for very large downward moves in the underlying equity, all other things assumed equal.

The issuer may find investor demand for this security because the investor is willing to give up some upside participation so that in the event of a downdrought in the underlying equity market, the floor sits only some 20 points below the current market price of the security. A measure to appreciate the extent by which the share price lies above or below the floor is the parity divided by the floor (S/IV). In this first example, S/IV is estimated to be 1.06.

ALTERING THE LIFE OF THE LOAN

We now consider the implications of extending the maturity of the loan. The life of the convertible bond is now set at seven years and all other factors are

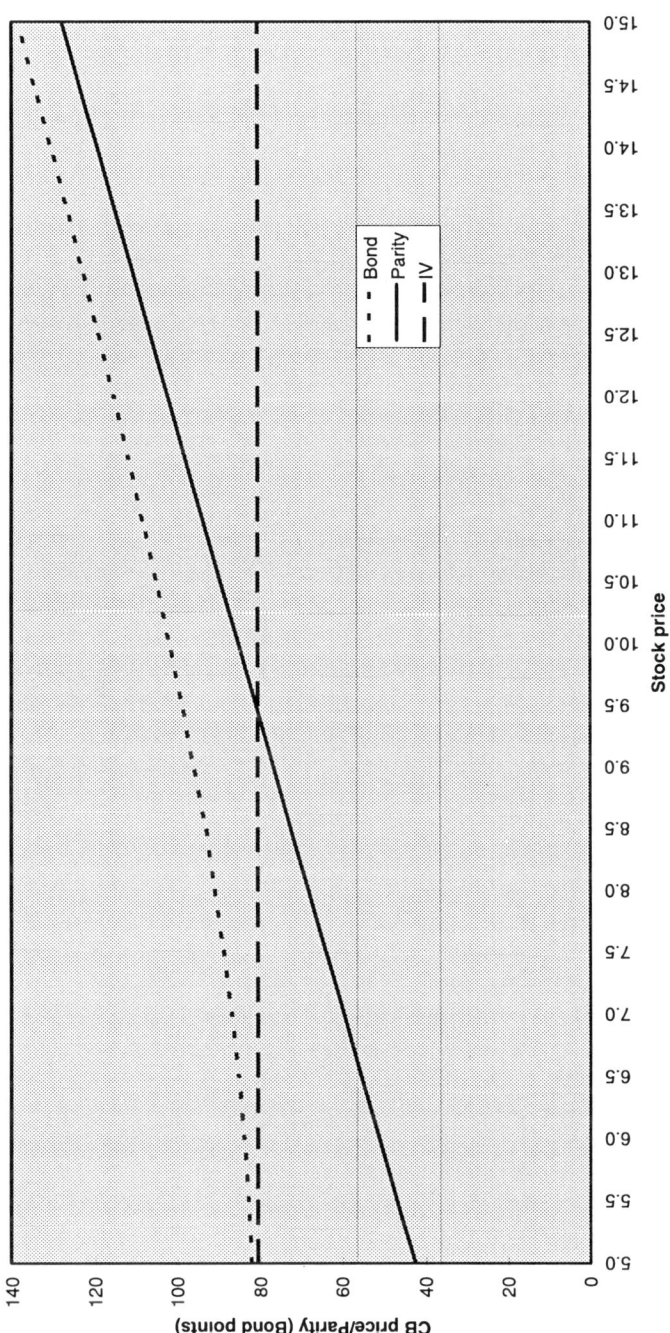

Figure 2.2: *Plain vanilla CB – 5 years, 5% coupon, 17% issue premium, 20% stock volatility, 300 bps risk premium, 3 years hard no call, no put*

Issue price:	100%	**Theoretical spread:**	300 b.p.
Stock price:	10.00	**Interest rate:**	6.96%
Conversion price/Ratio:	11.70/85.4701	**Investment value:**	80.87%
Maturity/Coupon:	11–Jul.–01/5% (A)	**Parity:**	85.47%
Call provision (Hard-non):	11–Jul.–99/130 trigger	**Yield to maturity:**	5.00%

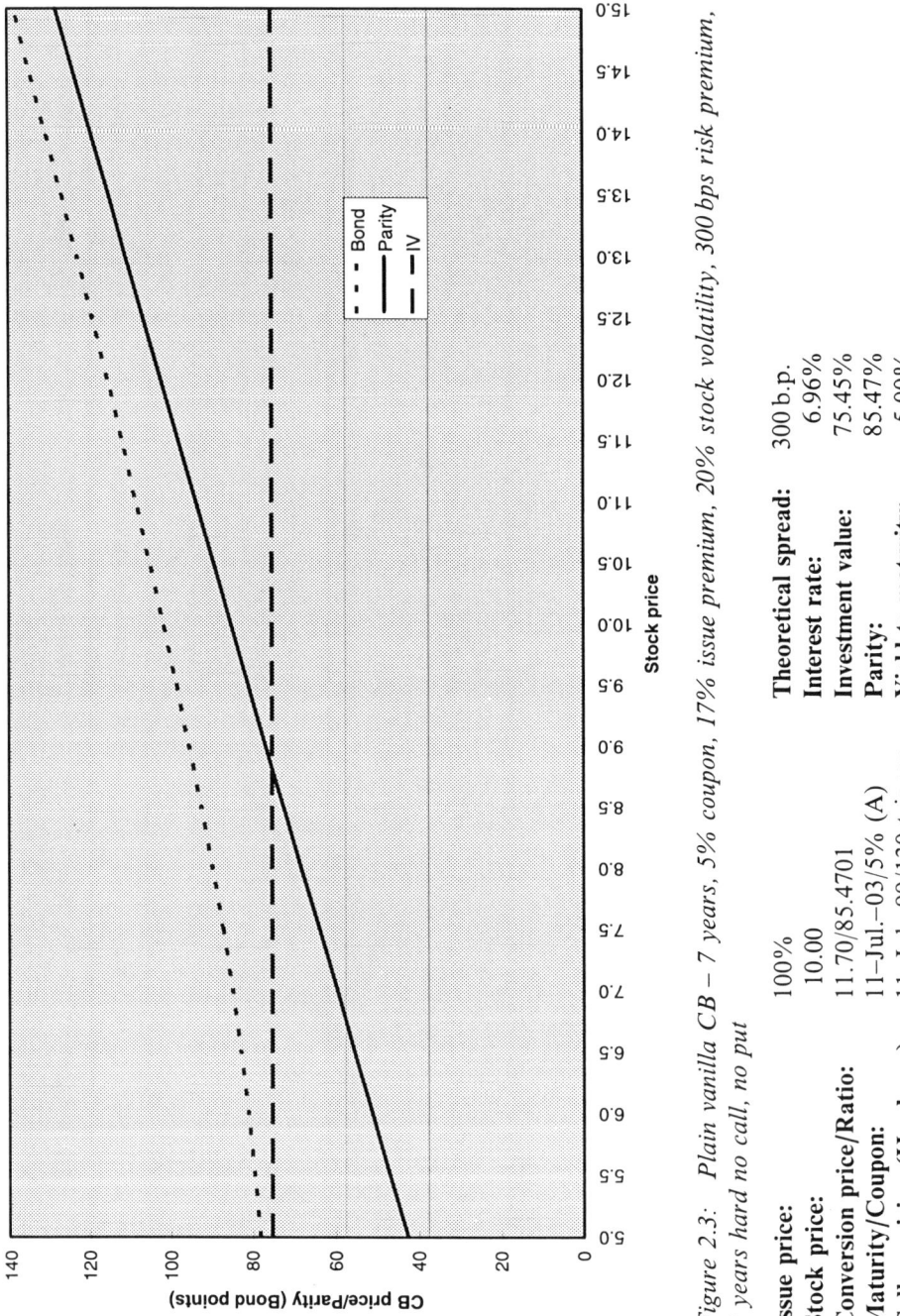

Figure 2.3: Plain vanilla CB – 7 years, 5% coupon, 17% issue premium, 20% stock volatility, 300 bps risk premium, 3 years hard no call, no put

Issue price:	100%	**Theoretical spread:**	300 b.p.
Stock price:	10.00	**Interest rate:**	6.96%
Conversion price/Ratio:	11.70/85.4701	**Investment value:**	75.45%
Maturity/Coupon:	11–Jul.–03/5% (A)	**Parity:**	85.47%
Call provision (Hard–non):	11–Jul.–99/130 trigger	**Yield to maturity:**	5.00%

held constant. Figure 2.3 plots our new bond. The important point is that the bond floor is now of course lower at 76.45%, which of course increases the level of 'in the moneyness' of the security. S/IV is now estimated at 1.13. The longer dated bond is more equity orientated than the five year bond – there is more equity participation for upside moves, but similarly the protection of the floor is further beneath current levels.

There are many occasions, say for example in Japan, where a company may issue half its debt as a five year deal and the remainder as a seven year deal. With certain characteristics, investors will want to pay more for the shorter dated CB because the parity is not as far above the bond floor and therefore the instrument is not merely synthesising equity.

ALTERING THE PREMIUM/COUPON MIX

Another simple way to alter the degree by which the issue trades on a premium is to alter the coupon. Effectively, by increasing the coupon, the bond rises all other things being equal. And vice versa for decreases in the coupon.

Returning to our convertible bond with a five year life, three examples of altering the coupon/premium mix are considered, in Figures 2.4, 2.5, and 2.6. In Figures 2.4 and 2.5, small adjustments in coupon rates of 100 basis points are considered down to 4% and up to 6% respectively. In the former case, the reduction in coupon lowers the bond floor, which means that the issuer has to lower the premium to 11% on the new issue to still attract the same investor demand. In contrast, when the issuer is in favour of increasing coupon payments to 6%, it effectively can issue a more debt orientated security with say a 25% issue premium in this case.

SYNTHESISING EQUITY

Let's now consider a more extreme example. We assume an equity which is paying no dividend. If the company under consideration was to reduce the coupon on the five year convertible bond considerably to 2% the bond floor falls to a level of 69%. The parity is now above the floor of the bond to such a large extent (S/IV = 1.41) that the bond is almost synthesising equity. Given share price increases, the CB captures most of the move in the equity. Most of the difference between the price paid for the equity and the price paid for the bond is explained by yield advantage or disadvantage as explained in Chapter 1.

Consequently, the issuer can no longer attract investors by bringing the bond with a very high premium. The premium is reduced to 2.5%.

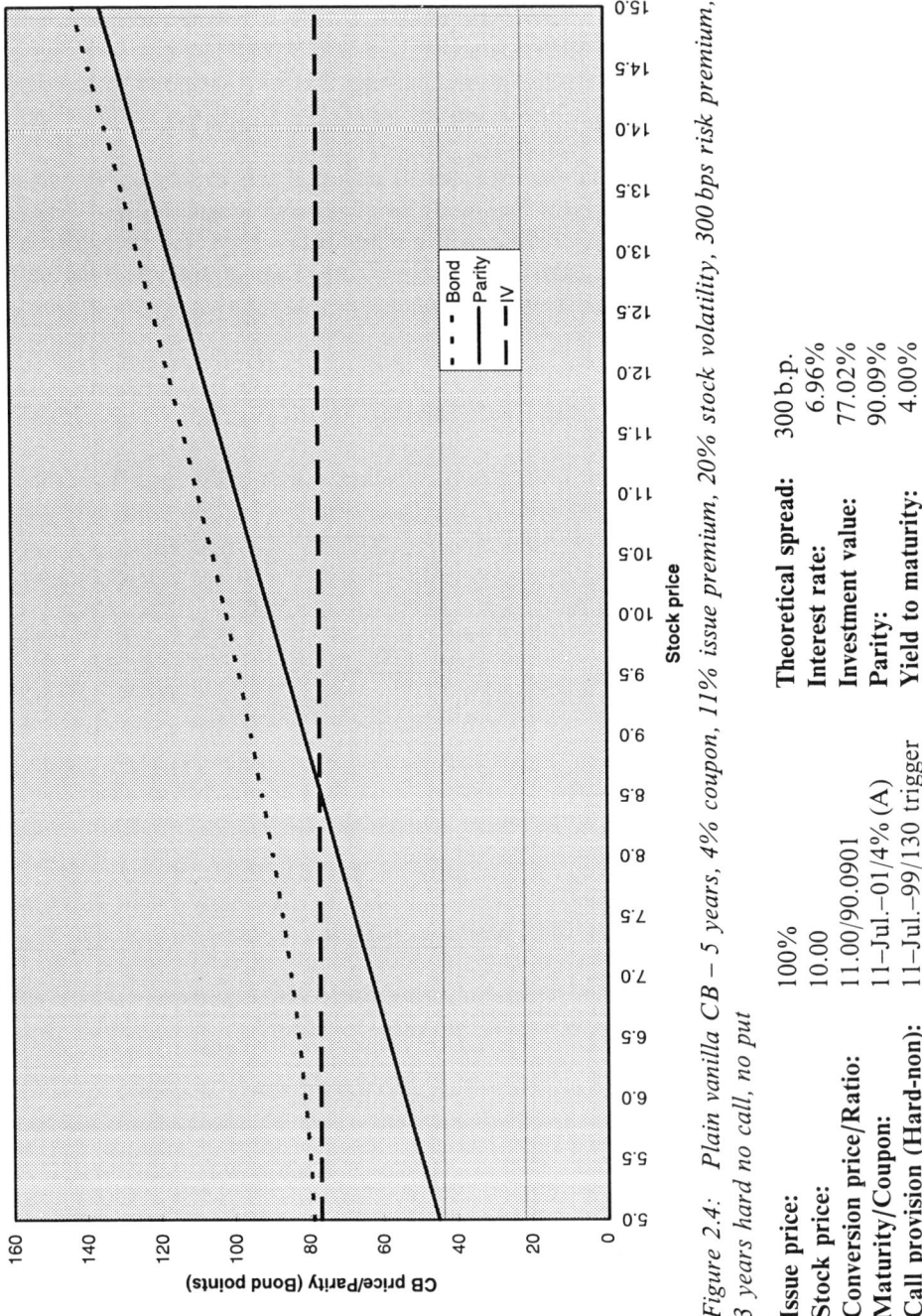

Figure 2.4: Plain vanilla CB – 5 years, 4% coupon, 11% issue premium, 20% stock volatility, 300 bps risk premium, 3 years hard no call, no put

Issue price:	100%	**Theoretical spread:**	300 b.p.
Stock price:	10.00	**Interest rate:**	6.96%
Conversion price/Ratio:	11.00/90.0901	**Investment value:**	77.02%
Maturity/Coupon:	11–Jul.–01/4% (A)	**Parity:**	90.09%
Call provision (Hard-non):	11–Jul.–99/130 trigger	**Yield to maturity:**	4.00%

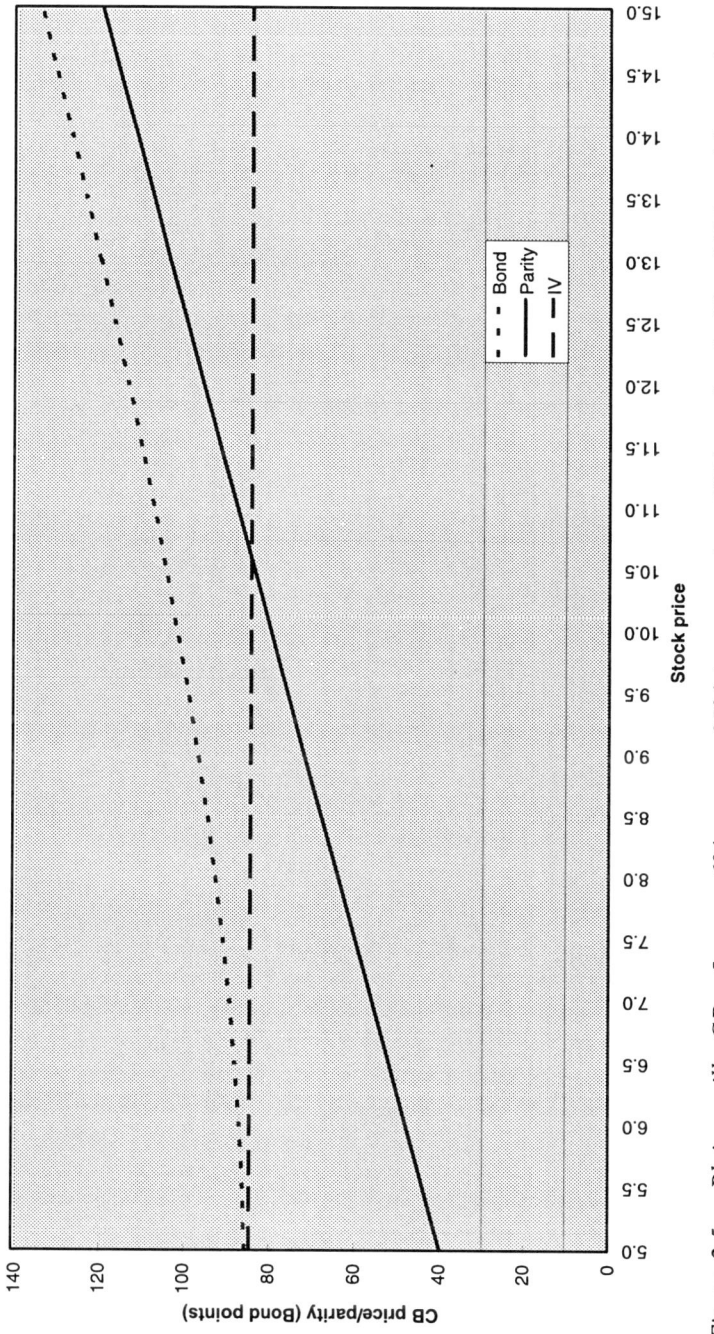

Figure 2.5: Plain vanilla CB – 5 years, 6% coupon, 25% issue premium, 20% stock volatility, 300 bps risk premium, 3 years hard no call, no put

Issue price:	100%	**Theoretical spread:**	300 b.p.
Stock price:	10.00	**Interest rate:**	6.96%
Conversion price/Ratio:	12.50/80.00	**Investment value:**	84.73%
Maturity/Coupon:	11–Jul.–01/6% (A)	**Parity:**	80.00%
Call provision (Hard-non):	11–Jul.–99/130 trigger	**Yield to maturity:**	6.00%

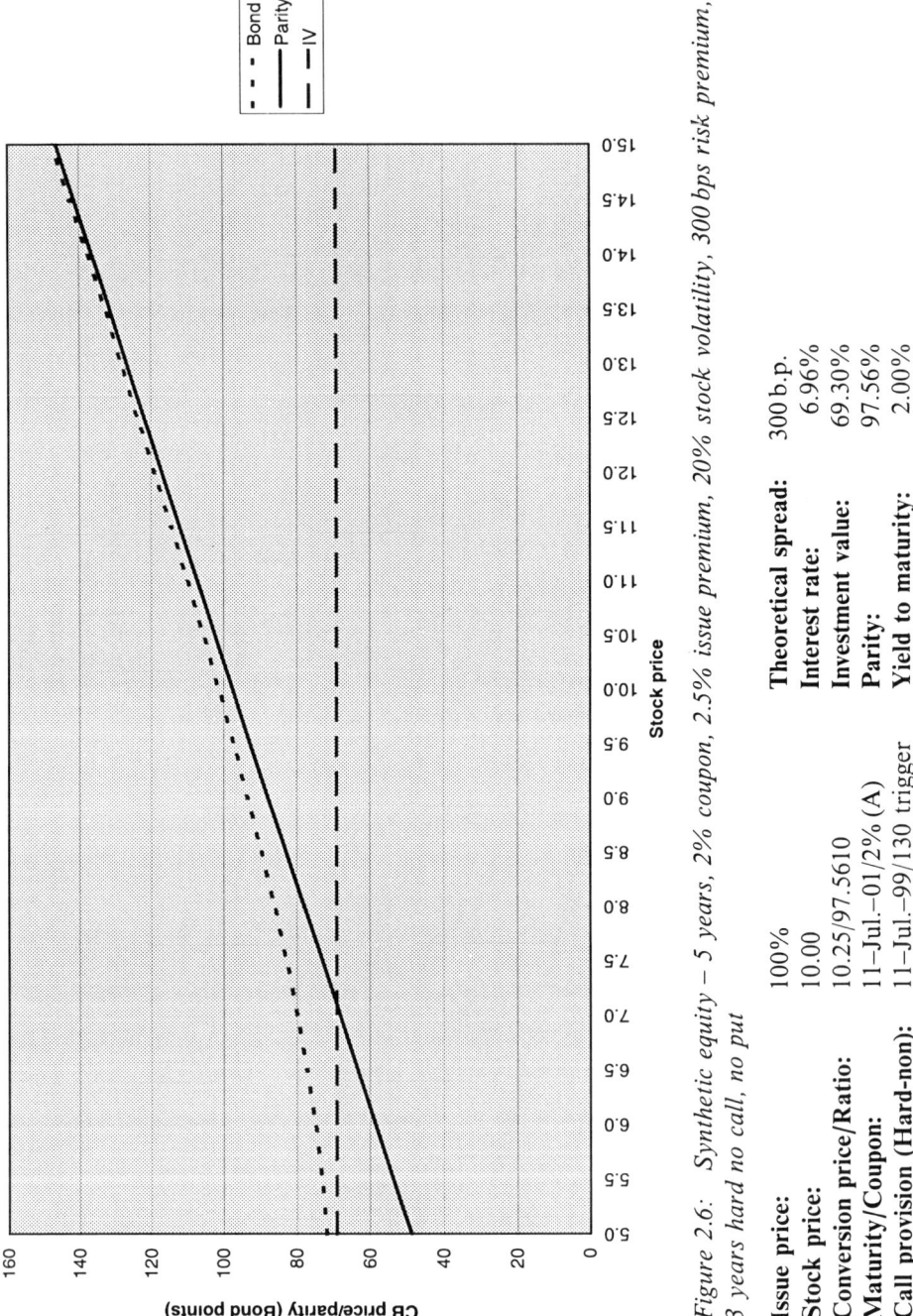

Figure 2.6: Synthetic equity – 5 years, 2% coupon, 2.5% issue premium, 20% stock volatility, 300 bps risk premium, 3 years hard no call, no put

Issue price:	100%	**Theoretical spread:**	300 b.p.
Stock price:	10.00	**Interest rate:**	6.96%
Conversion price/Ratio:	10.25/97.5610	**Investment value:**	69.30%
Maturity/Coupon:	11–Jul.–01/2% (A)	**Parity:**	97.56%
Call provision (Hard-non):	11–Jul.–99/130 trigger	**Yield to maturity:**	2.00%

PUT AND CALL PROVISIONS

Bonds often have what are referred to as 'call' features, which allow the issuer to repurchase the bonds at a particular price. It is generally argued that companies insert such clauses so that they may refinance at lower rates, but this argument is erroneous, as investors would pay less for the bond with this feature. The feature does certainly create greater flexibility in the capital structure of the company. If the market perceives that the company is likely to call the bond shortly, the bonds will reflect this fact and may trade at parity or a discount, reflecting the fact that if the bond is called and the holder is forced to convert, then no accrued interest will be paid. Call features reduce the expected life of the instrument.

A put provision is a less common option, particularly in the developed world, and allows the holder to 'put' the bond back to the company at a particular price on a given date. This is particularly relevant when a bond's share price is very low and will lead to earlier redemption when the bond has no option value.

The nature of put and call provisions and implications as far as valuation are concerned are addressed in Chapter 4 when we look at fair pricing, but for the moment we consider what it means for the company to issue a convertible bond with a put feature. The example we consider is a seven year bond, with a 4% coupon, 22% issue premium. However, in Figure 2.7 the bond is puttable back to the company after five years at 114.25. The put is set in many examples such that the security yields a given number of basis points over the benchmark US Treasury bond.

Note what have we done by introducing a put feature. The investment value of the security has been pulled up to 87.93%, but parity is now set at 81.97 S/IV now is below unity at 0.93, and the probability of dilution has been considerably reduced as a result.

ORIGINAL ISSUE DISCOUNT NOTE

All the convertibles so far considered have been issued at 100 or 'par'. This need not be the case. We now consider what are referred to as 'Original Issue Discount' (OID) notes. As can be seen from the accompanying data in Table 2.1, our convertible bond is now issued at 75 % instead of par, the difference between the prices providing the term 'original issue discount'. If the company raises US$100 million, it will have to repay a little more than US$133 million if the bonds are not converted. Annual coupon charges have been considerably reduced, and parity reduced. No capital gains is paid if held to maturity, with accretion-considered interest.

27

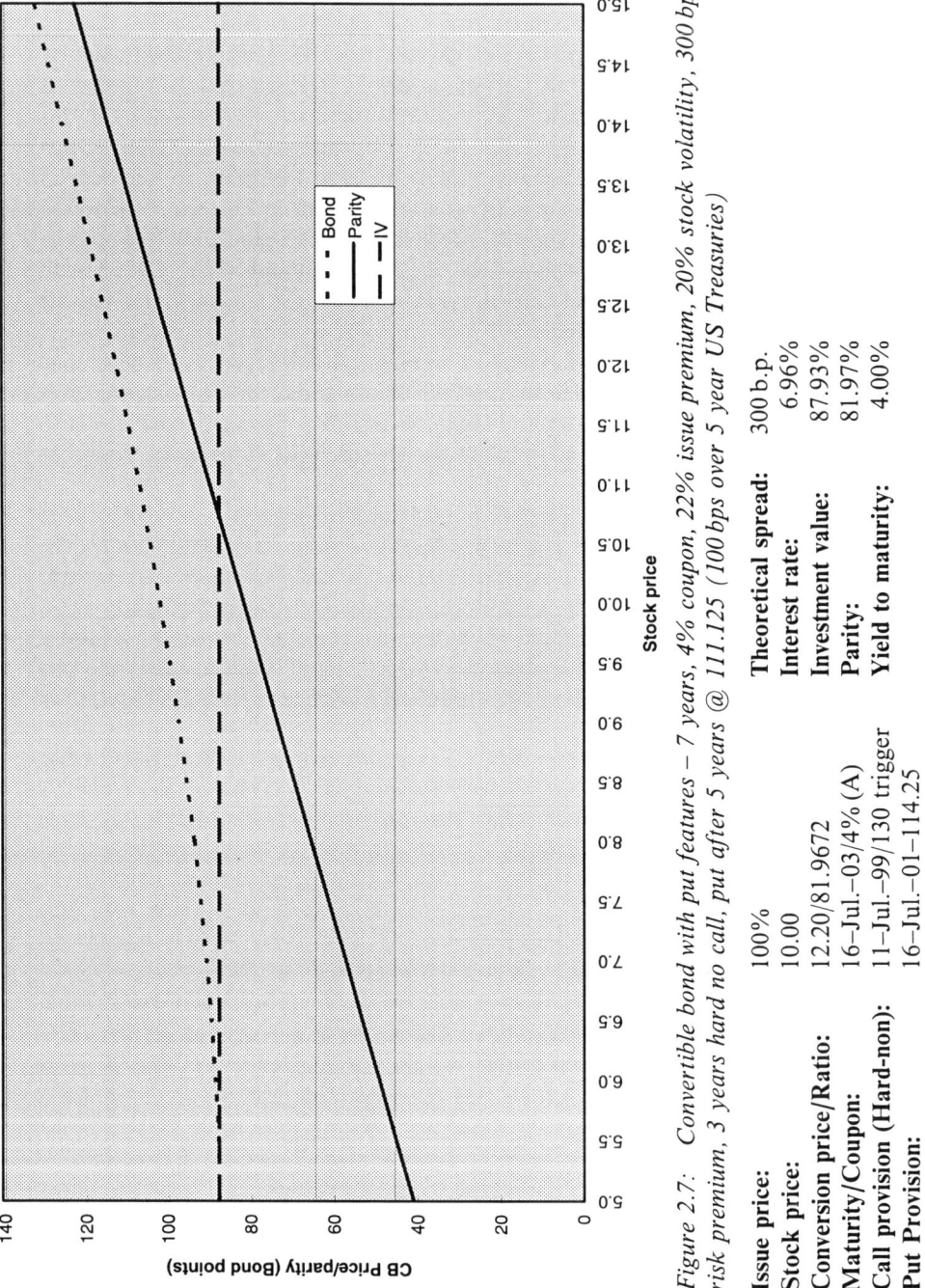

Figure 2.7.: Convertible bond with put features – 7 years, 4% coupon, 22% issue premium, 20% stock volatility, 300 bps risk premium, 3 years hard no call, put after 5 years @ 111.125 (100 bps over 5 year US Treasuries)

Issue price:	100%	**Theoretical spread:**	300 b.p.
Stock price:	10.00	**Interest rate:**	6.96%
Conversion price/Ratio:	12.20/81.9672	**Investment value:**	87.93%
Maturity/Coupon:	16–Jul.–03/4% (A)	**Parity:**	81.97%
Call provision (Hard–non):	11–Jul.–99/130 trigger	**Yield to maturity:**	4.00%
Put Provision:	16–Jul.–01–114.25		

Table 2.1: Original issue discount note (OID)

Issue price:	75%	Theoretical spread:	200 b.p.
Stock price:	10.00	Interest rate:	6.89%
Conversion price/Ratio:	12.00/22.2500	Investment value:	73.96%
Maturity/Coupon:	3–Apr.–01/2% (A)	Parity:	62.50%
		Yield to maturity:	8.69%

It is quite apparent that this particular CB more closely resembles straight debt than any of the other issues so far considered. The investment 'floor' is now 73.96 compared to a parity of 62.5, i.e. $S/IV = 0.845$. Probability of early dilution is therefore reduced via this type of deal. One can think of this kind of deal in stark contrast to the more equity orientated deals of, for example, mandatory convertibles.

EXCHANGEABLE BONDS

An exchangeable convertible bond may be any of the above types of convertible bonds, but it is issued by one company convertible into the shares of another. For example, if a large corporation has US$100 million of equity in another company (domestic or international) which it wishes to sell for strategic reasons, it may do so by issuing a bond with its own associated credit rating. No dilution will occur in this case, given that bonds convert into issued shares. This may be a particularly useful way for companies to divest interests in other companies. Moreover, the Italian and Malaysian governments have used this route when selling state interests in companies.

The focus of this chapter has been to show how both investors and issuers may interpret different types of convertible securities. To summarise, different structures can result in new issues resembling straight debt at one extreme, right through to equity at the other. Increasingly, particularly given the advent of more exotic type option structures, investment banks have thought of other clauses which shift CBs toward equity or debt. There are now bonds which have refix clauses and 'knock-out' puts, but all of these can easily be accommodated as will be seen from Chapters 3 and 4.

3: Payoff Analysis: A Primer for Theoretical Valuation

PAYOFF ANALYSIS

In order to gain a true understanding of convertible bond pricing, we want to focus on what is known as 'payoff analysis'. This will enable us to study what appear to be identical or similar portfolios of securities. For those not familiar with this approach, it may take a little work to really grasp the point, but we believe this to be necessary. Furthermore, it will be used on other occasions throughout the book.

Some of our readers will have a very in-depth understanding of options markets. Certainly most will have at least a basic grasp of these financial instruments. A '*call*' equity option gives the holder the right but not the obligation to *buy* shares in a particular company at a given price (the strike price) over a period of time. C is used to denote the price of a European style call option, S is the price of the underlying share and $PV(E)$ is the present value of the exercise price (E). The concept of *present value* is ubiquitous throughout finance and will be discussed at length in this book. To get the concept across at this point, consider a simple example of an individual who deposits $100 in a bank account, paying 10% interest annually over the next year. In one year, the value deposited would have grown to $110. The present value of $110 in one year, given an interest rate of 10%, is $100. We will also talk about warrants (W) below. A warrant is a call option essentially, issued by a company exerciseable into newly issued shares.

The property of option pricing to be first examined is that of American versus European options. We consider an American call on a *non-dividend paying share* until expiry and the reasons why it is non-optimal to exercise early. It might initially seem intuitive that an American option should be worth more than a European option since it provides all the same advantages as its counterpart, but also allows for early exercise. As already noted, however, this option is worth nothing more in this case, because it would be non-optimal to exercise early, as now shown.

Let's consider portfolio 1 which is simply a long call. Portfolio 2 is an investor buying the underlying share with no cash payments, having borrowed an amount equal to the present value of the exercise payment.

Of course, at expiry (T^*), the value of the call $= \max(S - E, 0)$. Let's say that our call has an exercise price equal to 100 and that the share price is 150 at T^*. At expiry, the holder of the call may pay an exercise price of 100 and receive a share priced at 150. The difference of 50 units is the terminal value. If the share price is below 100 at T^*, the option has no intrinsic value and is worth zero. When an option has a positive intrinsic value (i.e. $S > E$), it is said to be '*in the money*'. When the intrinsic value is negative (i.e. $S < E$), it is said to be '*out of the money*', and when intrinsic value is zero (i.e. $S = E$), the issue *is* '*at the money*'. The value of portfolio 2 is $S - E$, irrespective of the share price level in the second time period. This portfolio may then be worth a negative amount at T^*. The portfolios are therefore not equal, but portfolio 1 must be *at least as much* as portfolio 2 and so in order for arbitrage not to exist prior to T^*, it is possible to say that:

$$C \geq S - PV(E) \tag{3.1}$$

Table 3.1 explains why the concept of early exercise of an American call is not vital in this example. If the American call is exercised prior to expiry, the full exercise amount is paid in exchange for the share, i.e. $S - E$, whereas from the above it is obvious that the call should at least be worth its discounted parity value.

It is optimal to postpone paying the exercise amount until the last moment.

Table 3.1: Example illustrating minimum bound for American call

		T	T*
Portfolio 1			
Long call	*C*	$S <= E$ 0	$S >= E$ $S - E$
Portfolio 2			
Long share borrow *E*	$S - PV(E)$	$S - E$	$S - E$

THE ZERO COUPON CONVERTIBLE BOND

Now, much more relevant to the subject of convertibles, it can be shown at expiry that in the case of a zero coupon convertible bond,

Convertible Bond $=$ **max** $(S,$ **min** $(E, V))$ (3.2)

where E is the exercise amount, or par value of the bond in T^*, and S is the intrinsic value of the bond at expiry. V is the value of the firm in T^* in the case where the firm is unable to repay E. (Convertible bonds most commonly represent subordinated debt, with other bondholders taking priority over CB holders in the event of bankruptcy.)

Consider which portfolio would give exactly the same profile in time period T^*. Such a portfolio is illustrated below as portfolio 2, in Table 3.2. In the case of $S \geq E$ at T^*, the holder of a call option will pay out E and receive S (i.e. $S - E$). At the same time, it is assumed that the investor lends an amount equal to the present value of E so that at T^*, the overall return will equal $S - E + E$ or S if the share price exceeds the exercise price. On the other hand, if the issue expires out of the money, the option is not worth $S - E$ but rather 0 so that the overall return is E, as long as the bond issuer can repay the principal.

Once again, the circumstance of default is now ignored until later. It is therefore the case that for a zero coupon convert,

$$CB \geq C + PV(E) \qquad (3.3)$$

The interesting point to bear in mind is that prior to expiry, one is not having to pay the full exercise or conversion amount, but rather its present value.

This particular point unravels considerable confusion that often surrounds the analysis of convertible bonds.

Consider Figure 3.1. In this example, the present value of the conversion price is given a value of 86.02 and at T^* will be worth par or E. In this case, the

Table 3.2: Example illustrating terminal value of CB

	T	T^*	
		$S \leq E$	$S \geq E$
Portfolio 1			
Long CB	CB	E	S
Portfolio 2			
Long call lend E	$C + PV(E)$	E	S

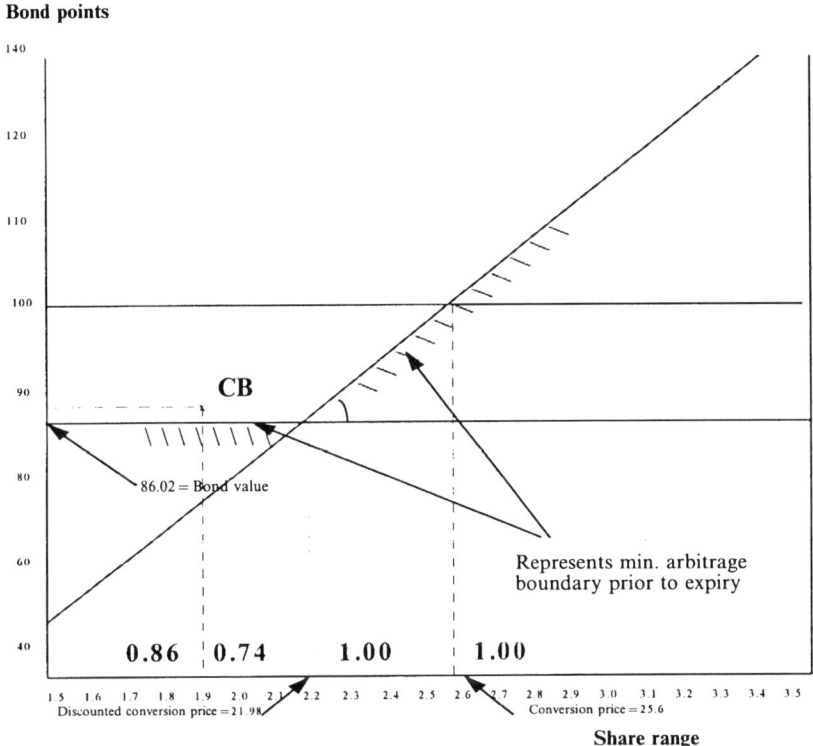

Bond points

Figure 3.1: Convertible bond pricing

bond value is 86.02. This investment value provides a lower bound for the instrument prior to expiry, when $S < PV(E)$. The 45 degree share price line shown in Figure 3.1 represents the intrinsic worth of the security, but if one wants to think of it being possible to decompose the option and straight bond component of the convertible for the sake of analysis, then S represents the discounted parity of the option portion :

$$\textbf{Parity of the option} = (S - E) \qquad (3.4)$$

$$\textbf{Discounted parity of the option} = (S - PV(E)) \qquad (3.5)$$

$$\textbf{\textit{CB} parity} = S - PV(E) + PV(E) \qquad (3.6)$$

$$= S$$

The first part of (3.6) represents the discounted value of the option's parity.

33

It is useful to focus on the components as outlined in Figure 3.1, in a little more detail. Prior to expiry, the '*kink*' in the profile is not exhibited 'around the money', but rather around the money on a discounted basis. The conversion and discounted conversion prices are clearly marked. The particular example shown is 26% out of the money (i.e. $S/E = 0.74$), but only 14% 'out' (i.e. $S/IV = 0.86$) on a discounted basis. It should be obvious by now that in the case of a convertible bond, if one wishes to exercise, one is in effect not paying the conversion price but more specifically its present value. Such bonds are said to be '*usable*', in the sense that the bond is used in lieu of cash as the exercise payment.

Consider now why it was relevant to focus earlier on the American versus European style options: what is particularly interesting is that if one thinks of

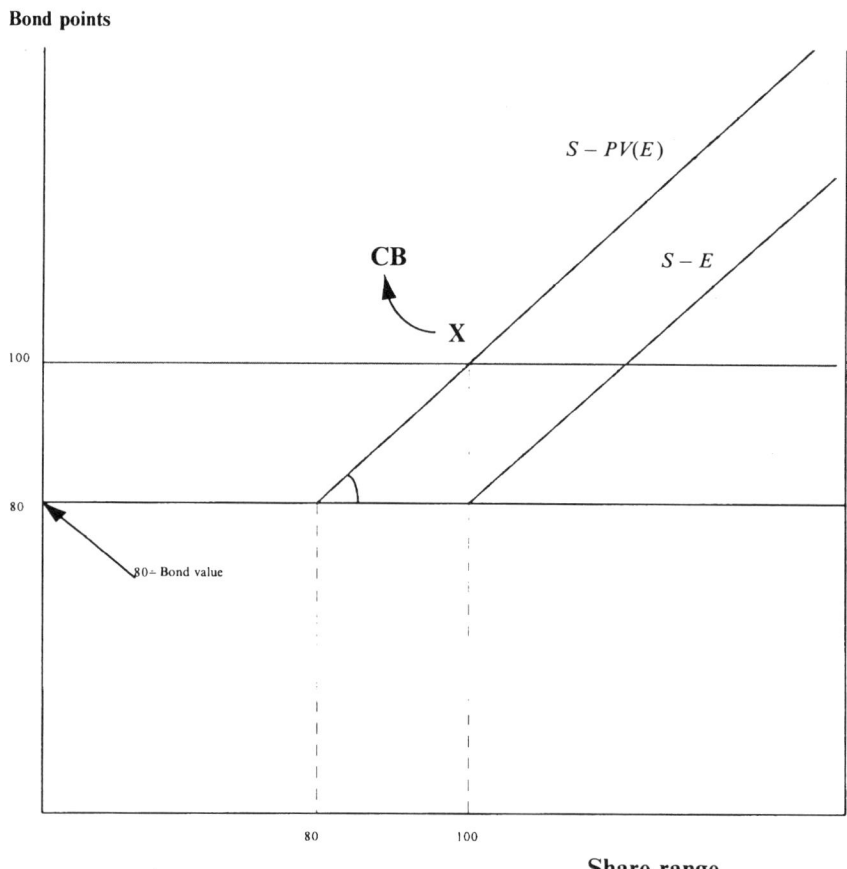

Figure 3.2: Synthetic convertible/convertible bond pricing

the separate parts of the CB, then by definition the option has to trade above $S - PV(E)$, where the discountedness reflects the yield on the bond. Let's elaborate on this by considering two examples, in Figure 3.2.

In portfolio 1, it is assumed that the investor holds a convertible bond trading at 100 which is also equal to the share price or parity of the overall instrument. The value of the underlying straight bond component is 80 so the option component is 20 by definition. In this particular circumstance, the bond must trade above 100, assuming transactions costs away, or arbitrage will ensue. To exercise the option, the investor has to outlay the present value of the conversion price, not the actual conversion price. The option component is trading at its discounted parity.

In portfolio 2, it is assumed that the investor holds a straight bond trading at 80 and redeems at 100, which is equal to the conversion value. At present, 80 is the present value of the conversion value. In addition, the investor holds a warrant trading at the money, priced at 20. Warrants are normally issued attached to a straight bond and are referred to as 'cum' in this state. Cum warrants have also often been called synthetic convertible bonds. The warrant in this instance is trading with zero intrinsic value. The total outlay has been 100. There are many practical considerations, however, which often make this synthetic convertible trade differently from the long convertible position in portfolio 1. Most importantly, just as an example, large proportions of Japanese warrants traded significantly below $S - PV(E)$ for over a decade, so although issues are being dissected theoretically at this stage, a depth of understanding can provide for considerable profitable opportunities which persist over very long periods. For example, with a share price of 100, it is not impossible for a warrant to trade at a price of 10, so that the cum package equates to 90. The warrant is trading at a discount to its theoretical price whereas, assuming all other things equal, if the convertible bond was trading at 90 worth 100 in this example, the discountedness would be exploitable immediately.

COUPON PAYING CONVERTS

We are now in a position to view the impact of coupons on the nature of convertible pricing. Figure 3.3 outlines the now familiar graph of a convertible bond. The bond in question has 2% annual coupon over three years and the rate at which we discount is assumed to be 5%. Relevant interest rates are 5%. The conversion price has been fixed at Yen 1000 for sake of simplicity and is denoted as E. The present value of the conversion price would be given by;

$$PV(E) = E/(1 + r)^3 = 1000/(1.05)^3 = 863.8 \text{ or } 86.38 \text{ in bond points} \quad (3.7)$$

35

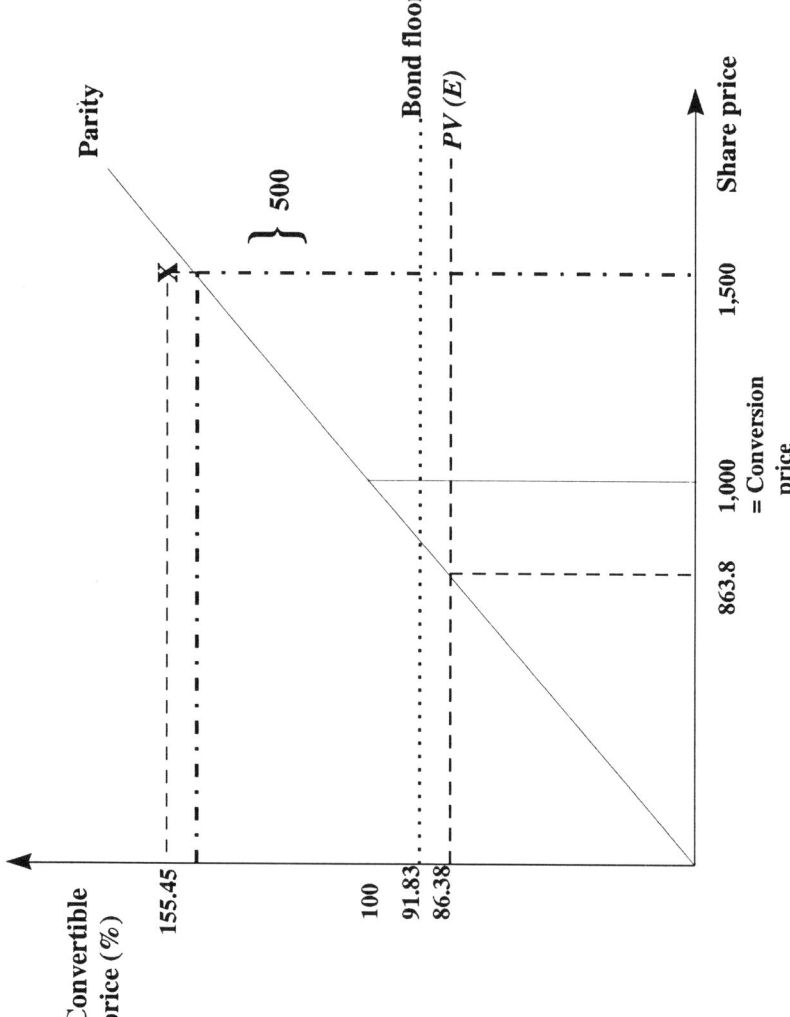

Figure 3.3: Discounted parity and the convertible bond

36

The investment value of this bond represents the present value of the conversion amount but also the present value of the coupon streams over the three year period and is given by:

$$\textbf{Bond value} = \frac{C1}{(1+r)} + \frac{C2}{(1+r)^2} + \frac{C3+R}{(1+r)^3}$$

$$= 918.30 \text{ or } 91.83 \text{ in bond points} \qquad (3.8)$$

where C = annual coupon payments,
     r = discount rate,
    R = redemption proceeds

Now, if the above was a warrant, 50% in the money, with the share price at Yen 1,500, the parity would be calculated as $S - E$ or Yen 500 as denoted in Figure 1.6. In the case of a convertible, parity is:

$$\textbf{Parity} = S - PV(E) + PV(E) = \text{Yen } 1,500 \qquad (3.9)$$

On the graph in Figure 3.3 this is represented by Yen 918.3 of investment value, plus Yen 500 of parity value of the warrant, plus Yen 81.7 representing the discountedness of the exercise price.

It is now apparent that discounted parity allows for the payment of coupons over the life of the instrument.

$$\textbf{Discounted parity} = PV(E) + PV(C) + S - PV(E) = 1,500 + 54.5 \qquad (3.10)$$

or parity plus an allowance representing coupon flows over the life of the instrument.

It is not surprising, if one studies Figure 3.3, that

Convertible bonds have been interpreted as allowing for equity participation, providing for downside protection whilst the holder has chosen to swap dividends for coupon payments.

The whole concept of '*cost of carry*' will be more formally addressed within the specialised field of arbitrage and hedging later in the book, but this has been a convenient point to reintroduce the simple concept of *yield advantage*.

4: Fair Value of a Convertible Bond

We did not initially intend writing so early about how to derive a theoretical or 'fair' price for a convertible bond. Such a subject is usually demoted to the latter part of a book so as not to put off the reading audience. But what is the point of writing a book on converts if it is not explained how to perform one of the most important tasks. It should be made clear how to price the instruments under consideration, so that investors may rank them, say which ones offer better value than others, or which ones are more suitable for equity participants, hedgers, or straight bond players. The fact is that we can spend the next one hundred pages raving on about premium and all kinds of second rate statistics, and all we will have is second rate results.

In Chapter 3, we really set the scene for this topic. We built up *minimum arbitrage boundaries* for converts, below which arbitrage was likely to ensue. We really did not develop an approach to help us clarify exactly how far above these boundaries the convert should trade in practice. That is the objective of this chapter.

FAIR PRICE

The first complete options pricing model was developed from the pioneering work of many scholars in the early 1970s, particularly Fischer Black, Myron Scholes and Robert Merton. The derivation of the Black–Scholes model (1973) from first principles is relatively demanding for non-mathematicians, although Sharpe did certainly make the model more accessible by outlining a straightforward derivation. Moreover, in *Investments*, Sharpe suggested a particularly useful framework for valuing contingent claim assets (non-proportional relationships between one asset and another), which was taken and developed fully by Cox, Ross and Rubinstein (1979) and now known familiarly as the '*Binomial Model*'. This is, in fact, the model that is developed in this chapter to investigate the pricing of convertible bonds. Most option type textbooks derive the binomial model or illustrate various aspects of the model. This chapter may show certain aspects of the model, but it is inclined to a practical usage. Moreover, it becomes relatively straightforward to show how complex features of converts can be easily incorporated into pricing. For example, call/put schedules, 'step-up' coupons or bonds with conversion price refix clauses may all be incorporated.

The fair price for a convertible exists where there is no opportunity to make an arbitrage profit. No view of the underlying share price is required. It is proposed that a riskless hedge can be established. Merton's *stochastic dominance argument* prevails throughout much that follows: portfolio *A* dominates portfolio *B* in time period *t*, if the return to *A* is not less than *B* for all states of the world and the return to *A* is strictly greater than the return to *B* for at least one state of the world. We touched on the concept of portfolio dominance in payoff analysis.

Before 1973, most approaches taken to value call type derivatives required the input of the future price of the underlying asset, or else empirical analysis mainly dependent upon regression analysis was used to determine which securities were more expensive than others. This was obviously not terribly helpful.

Convertible bonds can be relatively complex instruments. The price of a convertible is determined by a number of variables, the most important of which are as follows:

$$CB = f(S, R, T, D, C, \sigma, c, p, d) \tag{4.1}$$

where $CB =$ Convertible bond price
             $S =$ Share price
             $R =$ Interest rate
             $T =$ Time to maturity
             $D =$ Risk of default
             $C =$ Coupon
             $\sigma =$ Annualised volatility of underlying share
             $c =$ Call provision
             $p =$ Put provision
             $d =$ Dividend yield on underlying share

The convert may very well be a function of other terms such as conversion prices which refix.

USING THE BINOMIAL MODEL TO EVALUATE THE PRICE OF A CONVERT

There are a number of simplifying assumptions that may be made at this stage. Over the past three decades, many studies and academic developments have allowed for most of these to be relaxed. We assume that the stock under consideration pays no dividend, that there are zero transactions costs, or taxes, it is possible to borrow or lend freely at the risk free rate (note that lending or borrowing is the same as buying or selling bonds respectively), interest rates are constant, and volatility is held constant.

Let us initially also make the very unrealistic assumption that the share price can be one of two values in time period 2, $t + 1$. If the share price increases, it will equal uS and if the share price decreases it will equal to dS. We first illustrate an example of a simple risk free arbitrage using just a simple call option over one discrete period of time to maturity.

The share price can increase by 50% ($u = 1.5$) or can decrease by 50% ($d = 0.5$), with corresponding values of calls Cu and Cd. The exercise price is denoted E, and is equal to 100 (see Figure 4.1).

We know what the values of the call will be in $t + 1$ for both up and down states. If it is possible to construct a portfolio of Δ shares plus borrowing B dollars which mirrors the final payoff to the call, then we know that the call must be worth at least as much as the portfolio, or else an arbitrage would exist.

In order to solve for this, we establish the following constraints:

$$\Delta.uS + RB = uS - E \tag{4.2}$$

$$\Delta.dS + RB = 0 \tag{4.3}$$

In the example under consideration, the exercise price (E) is greater than the share price in the downstate (dS) and, correspondingly, E is less than the share in the upstate (uS).

Now we solve for the proportion of shares held, Δ and the amount borrowed, B.

From equation 4.3:

$$RB = -\Delta.dS$$

$$\Rightarrow \quad B = -(\Delta.dS)/R \tag{4.4}$$

Then, substituting (4.4) into (4.2):

$$\Delta.uS - \Delta.dS = uS - E$$

$$\Rightarrow \quad \Delta = \frac{uS - E}{S(u - d)} \tag{4.5}$$

Δ is the number of shares held and is known as the *hedge* or *delta ratio*.

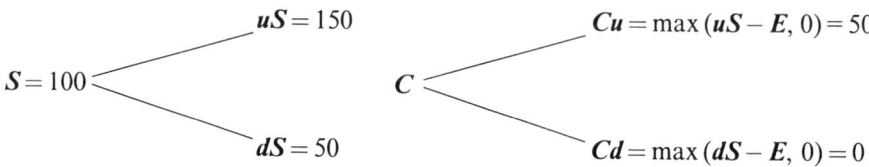

$$uS = 150 \qquad\qquad\qquad Cu = \max(uS - E, 0) = 50$$
$$S = 100 \qquad\qquad\qquad C$$
$$dS = 50 \qquad\qquad\qquad Cd = \max(dS - E, 0) = 0$$

Figure 4.1: One step results

Now let us solve for the borrowing component, B:
Substituting (4.5) into (4.3):

$$\frac{uS - E}{S(u - d)}\, ds + RB = 0$$

$$\Rightarrow \quad \frac{(uS - E)}{(u - d)}\, d + RB = 0$$

$$\Rightarrow \quad B = \frac{-d(uS - E)}{R(u - d)} \tag{4.6}$$

It must be the case then that in the one period case, the fair value of the call can be written:

$$C = \Delta S + B \tag{4.7}$$

In order to clarify the above, let's look at two numerical examples where the riskless interest rate is 10%, $u = 1.5$ and $d = 0.5$. In the first example, the prevailing share price is 100, and the conversion price is 100.
Inserting the various parameters, we find that:

$\Delta = (150 - 100)/(150 - 50) = 50\%$

$B = -25/1.1 = -22.73$

and

$C = 0.5 \times 100 - 22.73 = 27.27$

The investor buys 0.5 shares worth 50 and then borrows -22.73 which must be repaid in time period $t + 1$ with 10% interest (i.e. 25). If the share rises to the upstate of 150 then the investor has an of period stock value equal to $0.5 \times 150 = 75$ units. This amount plus the repayment of the loan equals 50 units which is the same as the call in the upstate. Similarly, 25 units is the share value if the underlying share declines to the downstate, so less 25 units of repayment gives a profile that is identical to that of the call and therefore must cost the same at the beginning of the period.
Now, let us impose the following constraint so that we may value more generally:

$$\Delta . uS + RB = Cu \tag{4.8}$$

$$\Delta . dS + RB = Cd \tag{4.9}$$

When solved as above, we find:

$$\Delta = \frac{Cu - Cd}{S(u - d)} \tag{4.10}$$

and,

$$B = \frac{uCd - dCu}{R(u - d)} \tag{4.11}$$

Let's consider an equally simple example of a call, but this time it is in the money in both up and downstates in $t + 1$. We have the same terms for the call except that the share price at the outset is 300 units. The share price in period $t + 1$ in the upstate and downstate is 450 and 150 respectively. Δ is 100% and B equals approximately -90.91.

The value of the call must then be equal to:

$$C = \frac{Cu - Cd}{(u - d)} + \frac{uCd - dCu}{R(u - d)} \tag{4.12}$$

$$= 209.091$$

If we write,

$$p = (R - d)/(u - d) \tag{4.13}$$

then the more general formula for pricing a call option may be written:

$$C = [pCu + (1 - p)Cd]/R \tag{4.14}$$

Let us come back to the first of the numerical examples again, but on this occasion we are no longer simply considering a call option, but rather a convertible bond with a principal amount of 100, a zero coupon bond, conversion price of 100 units and share price equal to 100 in time t. At this stage, it is assumed that XYZ Inc. bonds are default free. Now, from Chapter 3 we know that for such a plain vanilla convertible bond, the following payoff is witnessed for the up/down states:

Upstate	**CB at maturity $= uS$**
Downstate	**CB at maturity $= E$**

The final payoff to the above convert would be identical to buying a straight bond on XYZ Inc. plus a long 'call' with the same terms, all other things being equal (Figure 4.2).

At expiry, the convert will either be stock or will redeem, except in cases of default which are deliberately ignored for the moment.

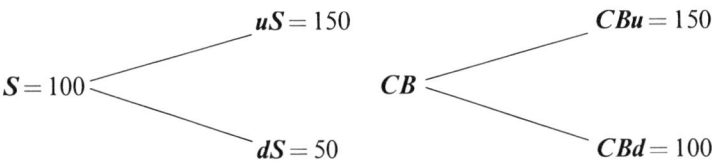

Figure 4.2: One step results for convertible bond

Now we can follow the process applied to a simple call option. A long position of Δ shares (50%) is established in this example with one interest rate equal to 10%. As in the first numerical example considered above, borrowing (selling of bonds) totals −22.73, but now we are in effect lending (buying bonds) equal to the net present value of the exercise price, approximately equal to 90.91. At expiry, in the upstate, lending totals 100, so that the replicating portfolio totals 150. On the downside, the proportion of shares held and the amount borrowed net out to zero but once again the investor receives redemption value on bonds bought. The profile of the portfolio then equals that of the convertible bond and provides for a simplified fair value at this stage:

$$CB = 0.5 \times 100 - 22.73 + 90.91 \approx 118.63$$

In the second numerical in the money example considered, the CB's payoff is replicated by holding Δ shares (Δ equals 100%) and B as before equals a total borrowing of −90.91. One is, however, simultaneously lending the present value of the exercise price equal to 90.91, netting borrowing and lending to zero. One is therefore effectively long one share then for both up and downstates considered.

Let's move on now to actually pricing a convertible in practice.

UNDERLYING EQUITY TREE

The first step in the implementation of the binomial model is to draw up the tree for the underlying asset, which is the common share in this case (see Figure 4.3). The share price shows what is known as a *multiplicative binomial process*. This is a geometric process which accelerates as the share price increases and decelerates on share price declines. Considerable academic debate has centred on the appropriate distribution to model stock price returns.

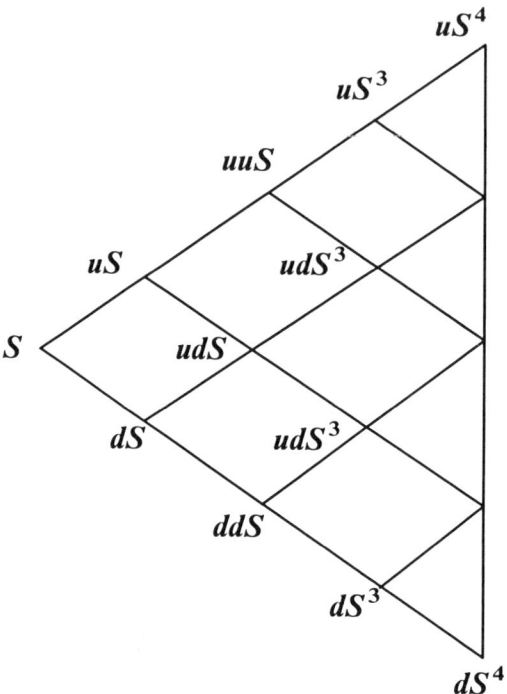

Figure 4.3: Underlying equity tree

The approach taken here is straightforward. S represents the current share price, which may take one of two values, uS or dS in time period 2. If the share price increases to uS, then in time period 3, the share price may take on a further one of another two values: uuS or udS and so on.

In practice, the following estimates of the 'up' and 'down' parameters are effective:

$$u = e^{r+\sigma} \tag{4.15}$$

$$d = e^{r-\sigma} \tag{4.16}$$

where $e = $ exponential, r is the riskless per step interest rate, and σ is the underlying share's volatility per step. Let's see how all the important parameters can be easily calculated.

Table 4.1 lists terms and conditions as well as estimated parameters which will now be described. Many of the lattices and examples shown below draw on this table.

Table 4.1: Using the binomial model to evaluate the price of a convert

Terms		'Steps'		Parameters	
Equity price	100	**1 Step**	0.506900	*u*	1.16756
Conversion price	100	Interest	0.012518	d	0.87820
T-expiration (days)	1825	Credit adj.	0.019883	*R1*	1.01250
Annual interest	0.025	Volatility	0.142400	*p1*	0.46420
Credit adjusted	4.00%	**Steps**	10	*R2*	1.01990
Annual volatility	20.00%			*p2*	0.48960
Coupon (semi-annual)	1.50%				
Principal amount	100				

Calls		Puts	
Year 2	115		
Year 3	110	**Year 3**	115
Year 4	105		
Year 5	100		

Table 4.2: Underlying equity tree

NS	0	1	2	3	4	5	6	7	8	9	10
0	100.00	116.76	136.32	159.16	185.83	216.97	253.33	295.77	345.33	403.20	470.76
1		87.82	102.54	119.72	139.78	163.20	190.54	222.47	259.75	303.27	354.09
2			77.12	90.05	105.13	122.75	143.32	167.33	195.37	228.11	266.33
3				67.73	79.08	92.33	107.80	125.86	146.95	171.58	200.33
4					59.48	69.45	81.08	94.67	110.53	129.05	150.68
5						52.25	60.99	71.21	83.14	97.07	113.33
6							45.87	53.56	62.53	73.01	85.25
7								40.29	47.04	54.92	64.12
8									35.38	41.31	48.23
9										31.07	36.28
10											27.29

Table 4.2 draws up a practical example of the underlying equity, priced at 100 in the present time period. The annualised volatility of the share is estimated at 20%. We consider a time frame of five years (or 1825 days). Ten steps are considered over the five year period.

Each step equates to $(365/1825)/10 = 0.5$ year.

The interest rate R is assumed to be 2.5% which when continuously compounded equates to:

45

$r = \ln(1.025) = 0.024693$

or per period,

$r = 0.012518$

$R1$ then defines the riskless rate and is 1.012518.

In order to view the annualised volatility broken down per period, one multiplies the volatility per annum by the square root of the per step time:

$\sigma \times \sqrt{T/NS} = 0.20 \times \sqrt{0.5} = 0.1424$

In this example, then,

$u = e^{R1+\sigma} = 1.16756$

and,

$d = e^{R1+\sigma} = 0.8782$

As an exercise, you should confirm different share values in Table 4.2. The tree is relatively coarse, but in practice, of course, the number of steps may be increased as appropriate. You might also consider what happens as you alter volatility or interest rate assumptions.

BOND TREE

Consider Table 4.3, which illustrates a 'plain vanilla' straight bond redeeming at par and paying a 1.5% coupon (semi-annually). Now the riskless interest is, say, 2.5% but an investor buying a corporate bond from this particular company requires compensation for credit risk or, say, 150 basis points, so that the relevant discount rate here is 4%. Ignoring default, all possible values of the bond on maturity are 100.75. '*Backward induction*' is then used to calculate the values at each node.

Consider valuing the straight bond at the ninth step or after four and a half years. At maturity, whether the share moves up or down, the bond will be worth redemption proceeds of 100 plus 0.75 coupon. So the value may be calculated using the per step credit adjusted interest rate as follows:

Bond $= (100.75/1.0199) + 0.75 = 99.54$

Table 4.3: Straight bond equivalent
Theoretical spread = 150 basis points
No calls or puts

NS	0	1	2	3	4	5	6	7	8	9	10
0	88.87	90.64	91.67	92.73	93.81	94.91	96.03	97.18	98.35	99.54	100.75
1		90.64	91.67	92.73	93.81	94.91	96.03	97.18	98.35	99.54	100.75
2			91.67	92.73	93.81	94.91	96.03	97.18	98.35	99.54	100.75
3				92.73	93.81	94.91	96.03	97.18	98.35	99.54	100.75
4					93.81	94.91	96.03	97.18	98.35	99.54	100.75
5						94.91	96.03	97.18	98.35	99.54	100.75
6							96.03	97.18	98.35	99.54	100.75
7								97.18	98.35	99.54	100.75
8									98.35	99.54	100.75
9										99.54	100.75
10											100.75

Table 4.4 illustrates the example now as a straightforward convertible bond with share price and conversion price equal to 100 in the present time period. Assuming that the share price in time period 9 is 97.07, then in period 10 the share can only take on one of two values: 113.33 or 85.25. We know that in these cases, Cu and Cd will be equal to the maximum of the bond's parity value or the redemption proceeds plus coupon, or 113.33 in the upstate and 100.75 in the downstate. Now we know the calculation for the fair present convertible bond value but what rate of discount should be used?

We do have a problem. At all nodes, should we discount by a credit adjusted interest rate when in fact this should not always be the case? First look at the

Table 4.4: Plain vanilla CB with adjusted discount rate

NS	0	1	2	3	4	5	6	7	8	9	10
0	115.93	129.01	145.04	165.36	190.45	220.63	256.27	298.00	346.83	403.95	470.76
1		107.73	117.02	129.59	146.17	167.36	193.49	224.69	261.24	304.02	354.09
2			101.35	107.88	117.12	129.96	147.26	169.56	196.86	228.86	266.33
3				97.37	101.58	107.75	116.85	130.06	148.44	172.33	200.33
4					95.51	97.98	101.59	107.14	115.94	129.80	150.68
5						95.27	96.75	98.62	101.29	105.60	113.33
6							96.03	97.18	98.35	99.54	100.75
7								97.18	98.35	99.54	100.75
8									98.35	99.54	100.75
9										99.54	100.75
10											100.75

corresponding convert price when the share price is 31.07 at step 9. The price of the bond is calculated on the basis that, at maturity, the bond will be redeemed whether the share rises or falls. The relevant interest rate to calculate what is essentially a straight bond with this credit risk is the credit adjusted interest rate.

However, this will not be the case if we look at the convert price corresponding to the share price of 403.20.

The hedge ratio at this node is calculated as:

$$\Delta = (Cu - Cd)/S.(u - d) = 1$$

One is essentially long of stock which happens to be paying a coupon. The risk-free bond can be synthesised by holding one convert and selling one unit of stock. Other things being equal, if the company defaults one is completely hedged and therefore the risk-free rate is the correct discount rate to use. It has been said that the risk-free rate should be used because there is 100% chance of conversion. This is not the case. One is at risk to the extent that one is unhedged, and it is that proportion that needs to use a credit adjusted rate.

One simple way to overcome this might be to use the following equation:

$$R \text{ adj.} = \Delta . \text{Riskless rate} + (1 - \Delta).\text{Credit adjusted rate}$$

All values of the convert at step 9 are calculated in this fashion, thus enabling us to continue the process at the earlier eighth stage, and to fill in the whole tree and arrive at a current fair price of 115.93.

COMMON EMBEDDED OPTIONS

Call Provisions

Convertible bonds contain a number of embedded options. In fact, the same often applies even to straight bonds. So far we have addressed the rights of the buyer of the bond almost exclusively, i.e. the right to convert the bond into the underlying share. The binomial model is particularly effective at allowing for 'what if?' at different junctures.

Let's now consider the most common provision allowing the issuer to repurchase the bond. This provision is referred to as the *'call'*. As already noted, corporate derivatives, and particularly convertible bonds, tend not to be normalised in any way, each of them commonly having specific clauses in

Table 4.5: Callable CB with adjusted discount rate

NS	0	1	2	3	4	5	6	7	8	9	10
0	112.20	124.42	139.78	159.91	185.83	217.72	253.33	296.52	345.33	403.95	470.76
1		104.72	112.96	124.38	139.78	163.95	190.54	223.22	259.75	304.02	354.09
2			99.27	104.81	112.91	124.99	143.32	168.08	195.37	228.86	266.33
3				96.21	99.51	104.15	110.75	126.61	146.95	172.33	200.33
4					95.20	97.36	100.32	104.52	110.53	129.80	150.68
5						95.27	96.75	98.62	101.29	105.60	113.33
6							96.03	97.18	98.35	99.54	100.75
7								97.18	98.35	99.54	100.75
8									98.35	99.54	100.75
9										99.54	100.75
10											100.75

the indenture relating to rights. In a considerable number of cases, however, the issuer may call the bond at a particular price, '*the call price*', in which case it will almost always have to pay the accrued interest since the last coupon date.

We consider a specific example of a call in Table 4.5. The call schedule is outlined and as illustrated, these discrete calls are often scheduled so that they decline over time. In this case, there is so-called '*hard non-call*' protection over the first two years of the life of the convert. That is the borrower cannot call the bond at any time before this time. It is also often the case that there is a '*soft call*': there may be a '*trigger*' price, above which the issuer may call the bond if it trades there for thirty trading days, for example.

It is almost always argued in financial literature that companies insist on call provisions for the simple reason that if interest rates fall, then the company will want to refinance at lower rates. *Prima facie* this sounds reasonable enough, but it should be obvious that inclusion of such a clause will mean that investors will pay less for such a bond. More plausible is the idea that without call provisions, a company cannot react to unexpected falls in inflation. There is no question, on the other hand, that calls give the issuer considerable flexibility in a number of regards. It might be possible for the holders to exercise sway over a policy decision so as to benefit themselves abnormally.

In order to introduce calls into the binomial lattice, certain questions need to be posed at junctures where calls may be taken up by the company. In these circumstances, analysts will normally assume that the issuers will act in their own interests and thus act to minimise the benefits to bondholders. Practical issues, however, will be brought up immediately after these are stated and illustrated, as well as suggestions for how such events may be better catered for.

$$S > X$$

Forced Conversion

This take place at nodes where the stock price or *parity value is greater than the exercise price (X)*. It would be optimal for a company to call a bond in this case because the option is worth more alive than dead. Let us take the first example of forced conversion from Table 4.5. Consider how we arrive at the bond price 345.33 which corresponds with the share price of 345.33 in step 8 when a call is instigated. The holding period value of the convert in this particular case can be read straight from the same position in Table 4.4, i.e. the fair value of the bond when there is no call provision. The holding period value is equal to 346.83. It is optimal for the company to call this bond because this value exceeds that of the security if forced to convert. So the company will call this bond at 105 and would have to pay the bond's accrued interest. However, this is academic since the bondholder will not hesitate to convert the security and gain the greater value of parity or 345.33. Note that the bondholder gives up any accrued if he converts.

If the share price is less than the conversion price, such as 35.38 in period 8 the respective holding value of the security is of course the straight bond price of 98.34. The company would certainly not call the bond under these circumstances.

The rule is that *if* the holding value of the bond plus coupon is greater than the call price, then the fair value will equal the maximum of – the call price plus accrued, or parity – *or else* it will equal the maximum of the holding value or the call price.

The non-callable convertible bond considered in our example was worth 116.68. The call feature reduced the value of the bond as one would expect by 4.48 points to 112.2. This is obviously just a simple example. There are a number of practical considerations to address. There has been much empirical analysis of call strategies, often quite conflicting. The fact is that it is unlikely that companies will call the security as soon as possible. In practice, share prices might be typically 30% or more above the 'trigger' price, although the conduct of companies does appear to differ quite dramatically from one country to another.

Most notably, as with many things Japanese, companies there appear to behave suboptimally. Even though most bonds have call provisions, it is very uncommon for the companies to call domestically issued paper even when it would appear to be beneficial to do so. Many reasons are given for this. It is our opinion that this is the case because of the complex cross-ownership of shares which exists. It would be perceived very poorly if a corporation called bonds because it would be most beneficial to shareholders, when many of the largest shareholders are banks or large financial institutions which also happen to be the largest holders of convertible bonds. After all, in Japan the convertible bond market is to a large extent a surrogate straight bond market.

In practice, of course, one should make assumptions that bonds are not called exactly at the trigger price, but rather at a level that is more reasonable given one's experience.

Put Provisions

Put provisions give bondholders the right to 'put' the convert back to the issuer at a predetermined price, the *put price*, at a particular point in time. As crazy as it might seem, we have seen investors completely miss the opportunity to put a bond back to a company with the result of a sizeable opportunity loss. In Table 4.6, a discrete 'hard put' is introduced in year 3 (step 6) at 115 plus accrued interest. Such a provision raises the effective bond value considerably. One therefore speaks of '*yield to put*', or '*floor to put*'.

The bondholder will put the bond back to the company if it is greater than the holding value of the bond. Consider the bond value corresponding to a share price of 107.8 in step 6. If the bond was neither callable or puttable at this point, it would be worth 116.85, as seen from Table 4.4. If the bond was merely callable here at 110 plus a coupon of 0.75, then the company would call, to maximise benefit to themselves. However, because the bond is puttable at 115, the holder will put the bond back to the company.

Table 4.6: Callable/puttable CB with adjusted discount rate

NS	0	1	2	3	4	5	6	7	8	9	10
0	117.44	127.11	140.50	159.91	185.83	217.72	253.33	296.52	345.33	403.95	470.76
1		112.62	117.62	125.80	139.78	163.95	190.54	223.22	259.75	304.02	354.09
2			110.61	112.77	115.75	127.50	143.32	168.08	195.37	228.86	266.33
3				111.32	112.77	114.24	115.75	126.61	146.95	172.33	200.33
4					112.77	114.24	115.75	104.52	110.53	129.80	150.68
5						114.24	115.75	98.62	101.29	105.60	113.33
6							115.75	97.18	98.35	99.54	100.75
7								97.18	98.35	99.54	100.75
8									98.35	99.54	100.75
9										99.54	100.75
10											100.75

VARYING PARAMETERS IN THE MODEL

This section has been included to give just a simple appraisal of how the fair price for a convert will be affected by altering inputs into the model.

Share Price

Delta
It should be very apparent that, all other things being equal

increases in the underlying share price will result in an increase in the convertible bond price.

The following simple graph (Figure 4.4) has been plotted using data in Table 2.4. When the share price is at low levels relative to the conversion price, such as 50 (i.e. 'deep out of the money'), the sensitivity of the bond to movements in share price is small. When the share price is at high levels relative to the conversion price, such as 150 (i.e. 'deep in the money'), the sensitivity of the bond to movements in share price approaches unity – the share and bond 'move one for one'.

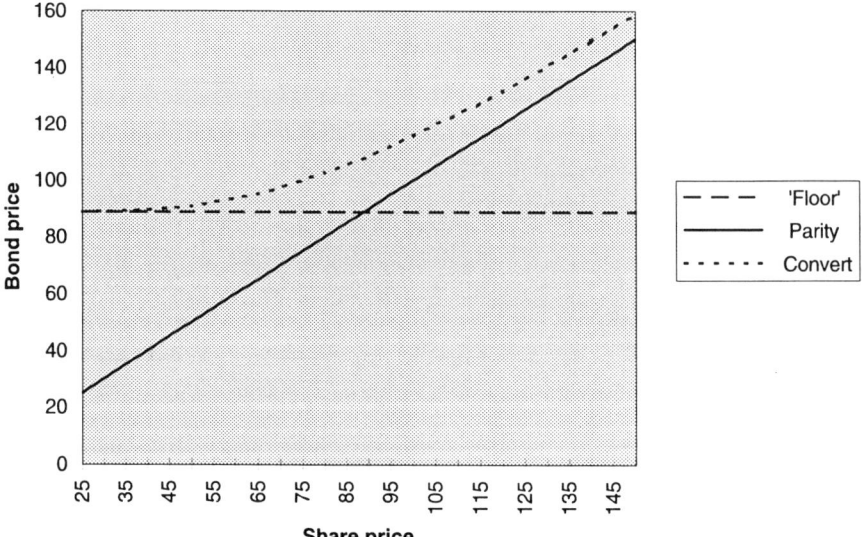

Figure 4.4: Convertible bond price curve

The change in price of the convert with respect to a change in the price of the underlying share is referred to the *hedge ratio* or *delta*:

$\Delta = $ **Change in CB price/Change in share price**

Specifically, delta may be defined as the first derivative of the convertible bond's price with respect to the underlying share:

$$\text{Delta} = \frac{\delta CB}{\delta S}$$

This is given by the gradient of the convertible price line as illustrated in Figures 4.4 and 4.5. At the high share price level, holding the convertible bond will feel like holding the share which pays a coupon in lieu of a dividend.

Much more will be written about delta when we come on to hedging. At this point, however, it is mentioned since it is relevant to investors of all kinds. Straight equity investors have always appeared so afraid of this particular Greek letter – 'it all sounds a bit too technical', or 'my job's to see which stock is cheaper than another, not to worry about the derivative'. It is of course

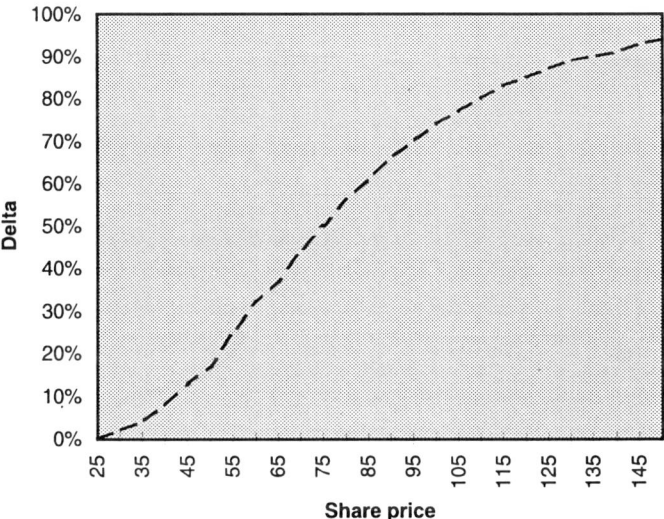

Figure 4.5: Delta function

53

crucial to understand the likely movements in the derivative if one is buying the bond in place of the stock, rather than being obsessed about premium.

Gamma

Gamma refers to the rate of change of delta with respect to the rate of change of the underlying share price and may be denoted:

Gamma = Change in delta/Change in share price

Gamma is depicted in Figure 4.6 and is the second derivative of the convertible bond price with respect to the share price. Note that at low levels of share price relative to the conversion price, gamma is very low. This makes sense, since if delta is close to zero and the convertible behaves just like a bond, then even if the share price increases/decreases by a small amount, the delta will not change. Similarly, at high levels of share price relative to the conversion price, gamma is low: if a convertible is deep in the money and the hedge ratio is one, then any small increase/decrease in the share price will not result in the delta changing.

Once again, a sound understanding of this measure is crucial when hedging these instruments and will be discussed at length later.

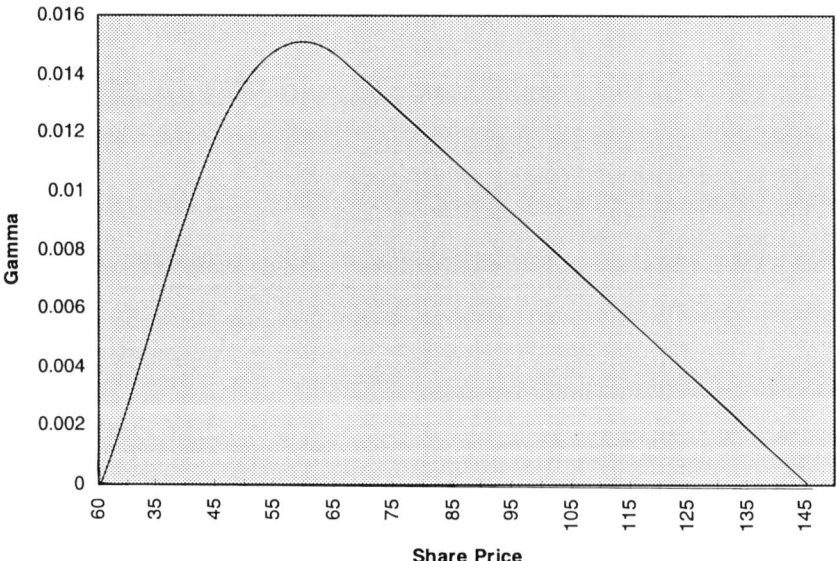

Figure 4.6: Gamma function

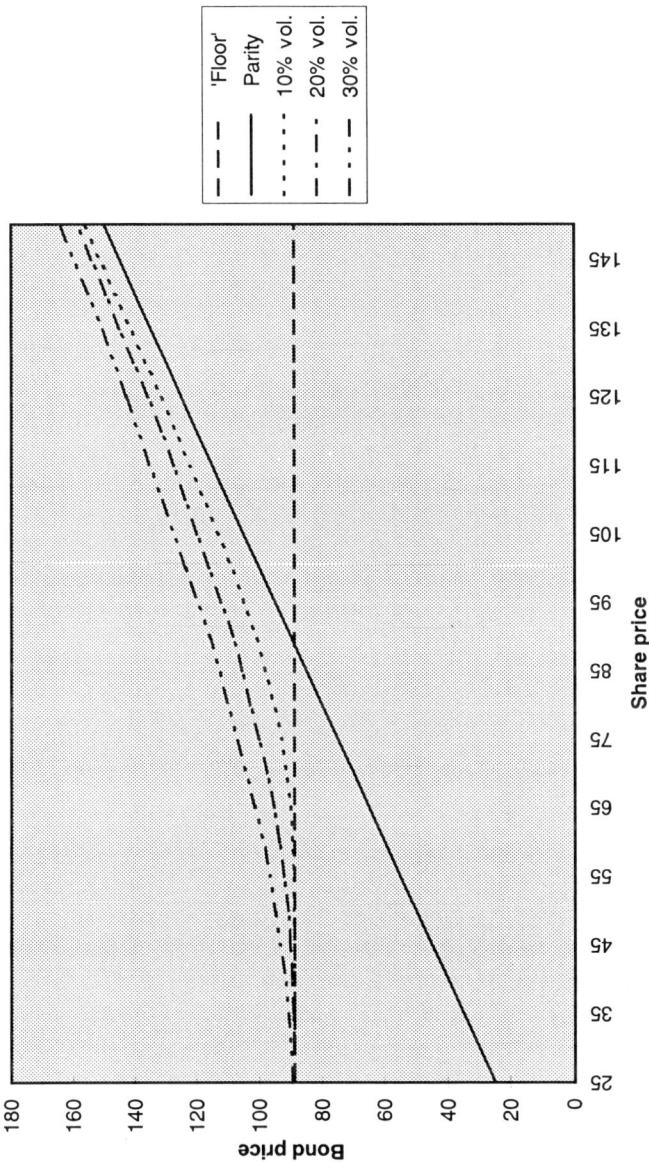

Figure 4.7: Impact of different volatility estimates

Vega

Vega is the term used to refer to the change in the convert's price as a result of a change in volatility of the underlying share. It is also sometimes referred to as *kappa* or *lambda* (see Figure 4.7). In a simplified way, one can think of an increase in volatility as meaning that the share has a chance of reaching more nodes on the equity tree. This will increase the fair price of the convertible bond now.

Figure 4.7 is a plot of our convertible bond with 2.5 years to maturity with assumptions of 10%, 20%, and 30% volatility estimates for the underlying security. Once again, we will return to vega, how to estimate volatility, and what the number actually means. Moreover, we will focus on *implied volatility*.

Rho

Changing interest rates impact on the price of convertible bonds (see Figure 4.8). *Rho* is a measure of the rate of change of the convertible bond's price to changes in interest rates. This is obviously very important and often overlooked by straight equity fund managers. Interest rate sensitivity of converts and hedging this risk is the subject of another chapter, but so as to simply appreciate the nature of varying this input, Figure 4.7 plots shifts up/down in rates for our convertible at step 5 again. Suffice to say at this point that deep out of the money converts are particularly sensitive to changes in interest rates. When interest rates rise/fall, the price of a straight bond will fall/rise, all

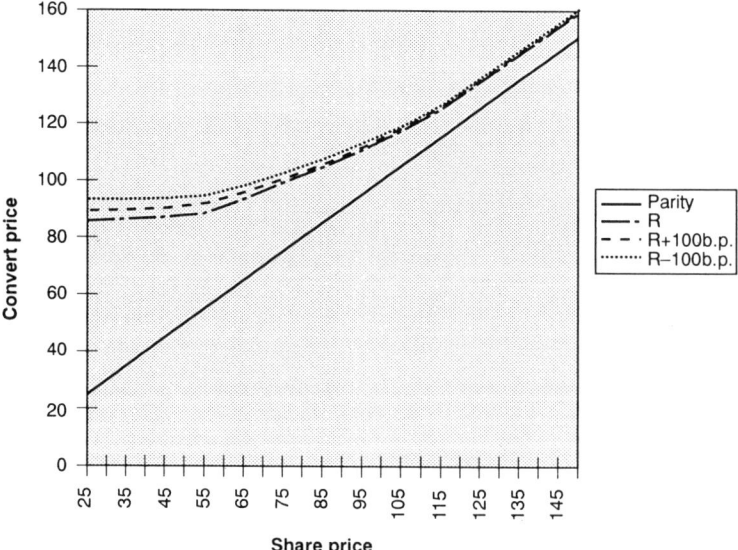

Figure 4.8: Impact of varying interest rates

other things being equal. This is exactly what happens to a convertible bond when it is deep out of the money. Deep in the money, however, where the bond moves much more like equity, the convertible bond is less sensitive and in fact may in many cases actually increase in value as rates rise, because of the positive impact on the option portion of the security. The sensitivity of convertible bonds to changes in interest rates is the subject of Chapter 5.

ALLOWING FOR DIVIDENDS

The binomial model can be easily adopted to incorporate dividends. At the time a share goes ex-dividend, it will fall by an amount equal to the payment. With regard to convertible bonds, it would seem sensible to assume a given dividend yield rather than an absolute amount. If this were the case our underlying equity tree would follow this process (see Figure 4.9).

CONCLUSIONS

As remarked at the beginning of this chapter, there is a tendency for some readers of books on options to pay very little attention to sections devoted to pricing the instruments. This is always surprising since no matter what the end objective, almost all practitioners will want to be able to see whether the convertible is cheap or not. This chapter has set out how to price convertible bonds, as well as showing how to price what appear to be complicated features such as 'calls' and 'puts'. Many readers with market experience will have an intuitive 'feel' for the likely behaviour of the instruments, but all it takes is an innovative lead manager to bring a bond with very different provisions and then suddenly there are many who are left questioning the significance of the

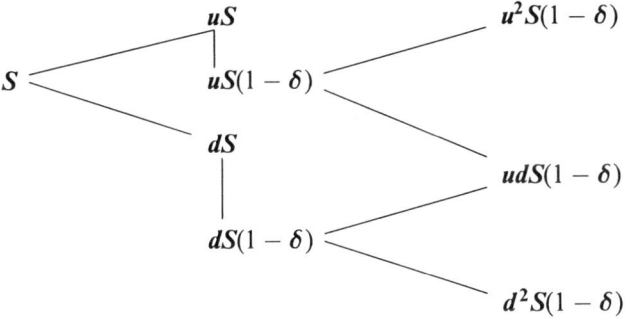

Figure 4.9: The underlying equity tree and dividend yields

57

changes. The algebra used throughout is deliberately fairly basic, and yet little has been oversimplified. Moreover, we have touched on a number of key areas which have caused problems when valuing the instruments in the past such as which interest rate to use in the model. Having derived a fair pricing model and noted various sensitivities of the convertible bond, we are now in a position to look at specific areas in more depth.

5: An Introduction to Interest Rate Sensitivity of Convertible Bonds

A convertible bond is a hybrid instrument. It has both a fixed income and an equity component. The degree by which it resembles either a straight bond or the underlying equity is largely dependent on how much the derivative is 'in or out of the money'. Convertible bonds reflect differing sensitivities to changes in prevailing interest rates depending on their equity or straight bond content. Before analysing the characteristic behaviour of convertible bonds, we will focus exclusively on the impact of changing interest rates on straight bonds, but even at this point it needs to be noted that one is ultimately considering convertible bonds (many of which have put and call provisions) as securities with 'embedded options'. This chapter provides a convenient place to at least outline basic bond theory and relationships which are essential for convertible bond practitioners.

The focus of Chapters 5 and 6 are risks relating to interest rates and credit respectively. Looking back to Chapter 4, it should be apparent that if it is possible to swap out the fixed income component of a convertible bond, then we are essentially left with a warrant, in which case therefore the interest rate risk and credit risk associated with the fixed income position of the bond would not have to be hedged. This may not be possible or desirable in a large number of cases.

INTEREST RATE RISK AND STRAIGHT BONDS

The price of a straight bond is *inversely* related to changes in interest rates, other things being equal. Given that interest rates rise/fall, the price of the fixed income security will fall/rise. This feature is referred to as market or interest rate risk associated with fixed income, and is of particular relevance to an investment which does not have the maturity of the bond as the horizon.

The price of the bond is determined by the present value of the expected cash flow. In broad terms at this stage, the following equation may be used to price the security:

$$\textbf{Bond price} = \sum_{t=1}^{n} \frac{C}{(1+r)^t} + \frac{M}{(1+r)^n} \tag{5.1}$$

where C = the semi-annual coupon payment in currency units
n = the number of time periods of payments
r = the yield per period
R = the redemption value

It should be quite obvious that the present value of coupon payments and the principal repayment falls as the yield increases, and vice versa.

The relationship between yield and price at a particular time is depicted in the form of a *price/yield curve*, for a given coupon rate and term to maturity, many examples of which are depicted in the Appendix on pp. 73–85.

Before considering interest rate risk, some further basic relationships are first outlined. The *term structure* of straight bonds is most commonly considered with reference to the yield curve which depicts the relationship between yield and maturity. Three points are most often referred to when explaining the yield curve.

LIQUIDITY PREFERENCE THEORY

The argument is that yields should increase with maturity because longer maturity instruments have greater market risk and consequently less liquidity. This is by far the most often referred to reason for a yield curve to be sloped *normally*. This is depicted in Figure 5.1.

This theory argues that the market will not view a one year bond and say a ten year bond as perfect substitutes, since although the investments may well have the same expected value, the longer bond will have considerably more market risk over the next year if interest rates rise or fall substantially, and so more risk averse investors may view the longer bond with a risk premium.

EXPECTATIONS

The *expectations theory* of term structure is not incompatible with liquidity preference outlined already. In selecting an investment in a straight bond

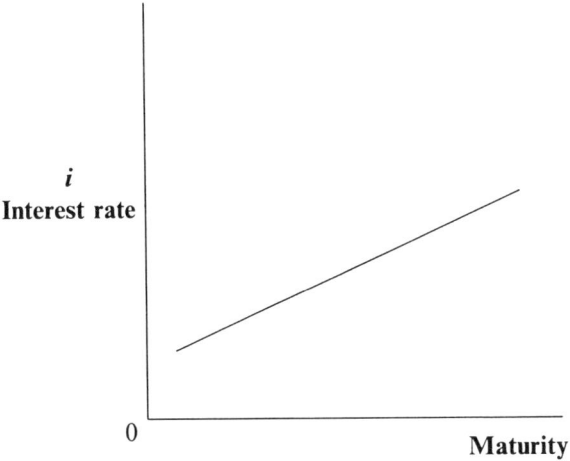

Figure 5.1: Liquidity preference and the yield curve

over a number of periods, an investor will consider investing in one security or a reinvestment approach – the approach with the higher expected return will be chosen. The heart of this theory states that the average of actual and expected short term rates will be equal to the long term rate. If interest rates are expected to be stable with future short term rates anticipated to equal current actual short term rates, the yield curve is 'flat', as shown in Figure 5.2.

If interest rates are expected to decrease, the argument is that investors will prefer longer term instruments as they try to benefit from higher interest rates prior to a decrease and in addition, this will provide for a capital gain. Moreover, borrowers will issue shorter debt prior to issuing long term debt upon a decrease in rates. This would cause the curve to '*invert*', as outlined again in Figure 5.2.

If rates were expected to increase, the reverse argument would provide for a so-called 'normal yield curve'.

SEGMENTATION THEORY

This theory argues that groups are constrained to invest in only small parts or segments of the yield curve. For example, pension funds and insurance companies tend to have a bias toward longer term maturities versus

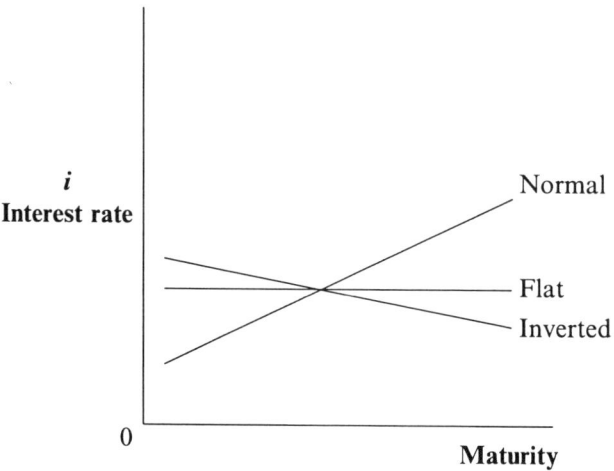

Figure 5.2: Expectations and differing yield curve characteristics

commercial banks, preference for shorter term securities. This theory is incompatible with the expectations hypothesis already outlined.

Simply to give readers an appreciation of what yield curves might look like in practice at any particular point in time, the US Government and South African Government yield curves are plotted in Figures 5.3(a) and 5.3(b) respectively.

DURATION

Duration is often used to measure the price sensitivity of a bond to shifts in the yield curve. It is determined by cash flows. Macaulay's duration is more specifically the *'weighted average time to cash flow payment'* (first formulated by Frederick Macaulay in 1938)

$$\textbf{Macaulay's duration} = \sum \{[PV(CFt)/TPV] \times t\} \qquad (5.2)$$

where $PV(CFt)$ = the present value of the nominal cash flow received in year 't'
TPV = the total present value of all of the bond's future cash flows
t = time remaining until the receipt of cash flow Cft

A number of factors affect the duration of a bond, some of which are outlined below (see also Table 5.1):

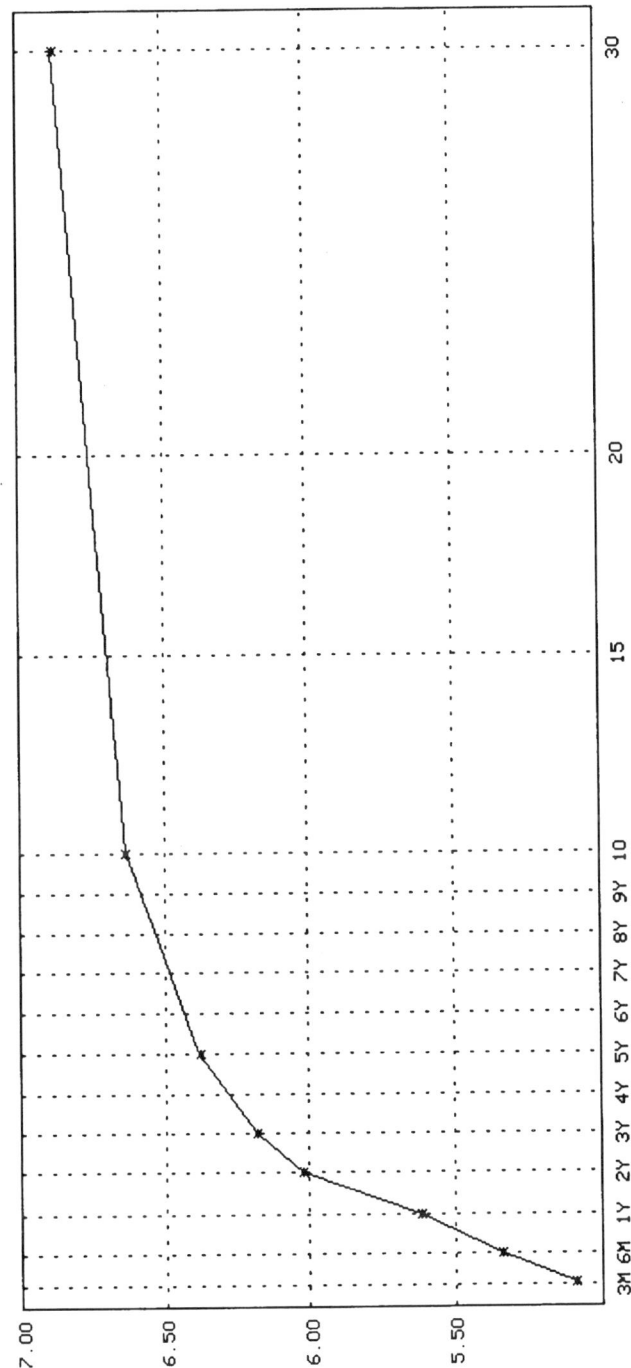

Figure 5.3a: Yield curve – US Treasury (range 3 m – 30; date: 10/2/96)
Source: Bloomberg L.P.

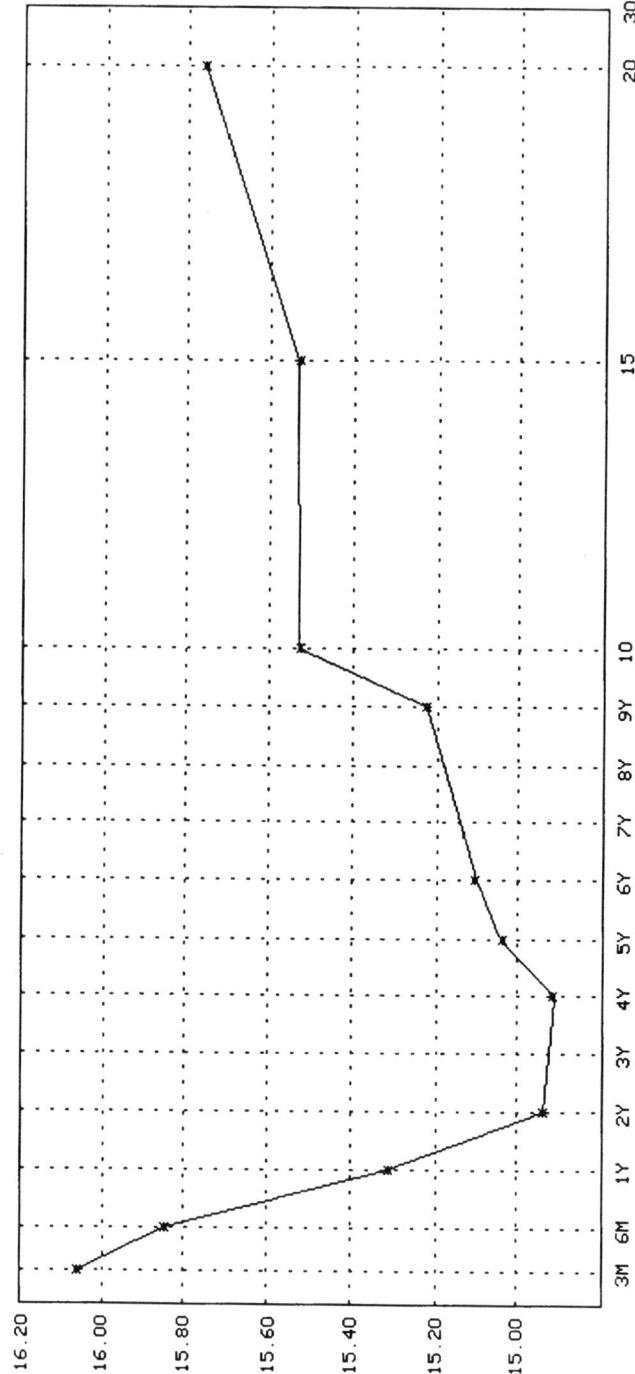

Figure 5.3b: Yield curve – South African Government (range 3 m – 20; date: 10/2/96)
Source: Bloomberg L.P.

(a) Term to maturity – *Positively related*, but at a decreasing rate: reasons include the fact that redemption is a large factor determining a bond's price, and a large proportion of cash flows occur after short term securities have already matured.
(b) Coupon rate – *Negatively related*: high coupons imply larger cash flows before maturity as well as the discounting process having less effect on early cash flows.
(c) Market Yield – *Negatively related*.
(d) *Sinking Fund Provisions and Call Provisions – Inversely related*: by lowering the average maturity of the principal payment.

US Treasury 10%, due October 25 1996. On 25 October 1994, the bond was priced at par (i.e. $1,000) to yield 10% to maturity.

The duration in this case is 1.8656 years. The duration of a bond will always be less than the redemption period except in the case of a zero coupon bond, when all cash flows come through at the end of the bond's life.

Modified duration is a measure of the percentage change in a bond as a result of a given change in interest rates, and can be measured as follows:

Modified duration = Macaulay duration/$(1 + r/k)$ (5.3)

$$= 1.8656/1.05 = 1.7776 \text{ years}$$

Straight bonds with the same duration will exhibit the same sensitivity to changes in interest rates for *very small changes* in interest rates. As far as we are concerned there are two important measures which we need to focus on when assessing the interest rate risk associated with fixed income. One can first consider the first derivative of the price/yield curve as giving the following:

$$\textbf{Rho} = \frac{\delta p}{\delta r} \qquad\qquad (5.4)$$

Table 5.1: Duration

t years	Cash flow	PV Factor	PV(CFt)	Weight	t × Weight
0.5	50	0.9524	47.62	0.0476	0.0238
1.0	50	0.9091	45.45	0.0454	0.0454
1.5	50	0.8658	43.29	0.0432	0.0648
2.0	50	0.8246	865.80	0.8658	1.7316
			$1000.00	1.0000	1.8656

which is a measure of the change in the bond price (δp) for infinitesimal changes in interest rates (δr).

The price/yield curve is obviously not linear and therefore rho is only accurate over small changes in interest rates. One therefore needs to be aware of the second derivative of the bond yield curve, often analysed with reference to a term known as *'convexity'*, referring to the rate of change of rho with respect to changes in interest rates.

$$\textbf{Convexity} = \frac{\delta p^2}{\delta r^2} \tag{5.5}$$

The Appendix considers bonds with four different maturities: one year, five years, ten years and twenty years. The price relationship is then depicted for the five maturities assuming coupon rates differing from 1% to 10%. Approximations of rho can be found in the raw data and graphs of $\delta p/\delta r$, and represent interest rate risk in bond points, assuming relatively large moves of fifty basis points.

Interest rate risk may be defined as an unexpected shift of the yield curve. Let's say a bond is priced at 130 and has an 'effective duration' of 10 years. If r increases by 1% the price of the bond would fall by $0.001 \times 10 \times 130 = \$1.30$.

It is commonplace for many corporate bonds to have call and put provisions, and as shown in Chapter 4 these provisions affect the price/yield relationship and therefore have a bearing on the interest rate sensitivity of the instrument under consideration.

INTEREST RATE RISK AND CONVERTIBLE BONDS

Figure 5.4 illustrates a hypothetical convertible bond's pricing. When the current share price is considerably beneath the conversion price ('deep out of the money'), the option feature of the convertible bond has very little value and therefore the instrument will trade very much like fixed income. On the other hand, when the share price is considerably above the conversion price ('deep in the money'), the convertible bond will trade just like the underlying equity.

If we were looking to hedge away interest rate and default risk entirely for a given convertible bond, it would be ideal to short an exact equivalent straight bond as that inherent in the convertible. This may not be possible in many instances. However, effectively the same thing can be captured by an investor selling the convertible to a party that 'swaps' fixed for floating rate and thereby obliges himself to issue a 'covered' warrant to our investor.

Because a convertible has a fixed income component, some aspects of the above sections on interest rate risk are more relevant. Many convertibles tend to have long dated option components and in such cases one of the most

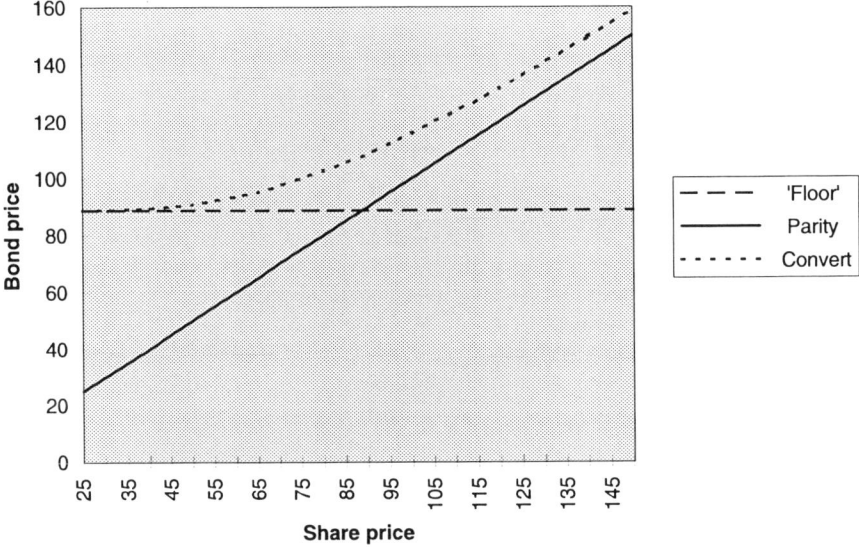

Figure 5.4: Convertible bond pricing

important determinants of their price will be interest rates. The option component of the convert is now positively related to interest rates, not negatively as is the case with a straight bond or indeed its own straight bond element, for changes in interest rates.

Most analysis of convertible bonds focuses on the fact that r is a key determinant of its price. We might think of the measure of interest rate sensitivity of a convert as measured by Rho in the same way as delta:

$$\text{delta} = \frac{\text{Change in convert price}}{\text{Change in share price}}$$

$$\text{rho} = \frac{\text{Change in convert price}}{\text{Change in interest rate}}$$

For the sake of simplicity it is useful to consider some examples of the behaviour of a convertible for changes of, say, 100 basis points up and down in interest rates, using a valuation model. The fixed and current terms are just assumed for this hypothetical example (see Table 5.2).

Table 5.2: XYZ Corp., 1.5% (semi-annual) five year CB

Conversion price	:	100
Volatility	:	20%
Interest rate	:	2.5%
Theoretical spread	:	150 basis points

With the issue 'deep in the money' i.e. Share price = 150:

Fair value	:	158.56 ($r = 2.5\%$)
Fair value *	:	157.67 ($r1 = +100$ basis points)
Fair value **	:	159.53 ($r2 = -100$ basis points)

With the issue trading with share close to discounted conversion price:

Share price	:	88
Fair value	:	106.99
Fair value*	:	105.10
Fair value**	:	109.85

With the issue trading 'deep out of the money':

Share price	:	50
Fair value	:	90.72
Fair value*	:	87.33
Fair value **	:	94.74

The behaviour of this hypothetical convertible bond given interest rate changes is as one would expect. Deeper in the money, the instrument behaves more and more like equity and deeper out of the money, it increasingly resembles fixed income. Realistically, when deep in the money, the whole question of interest rate sensitivity might be better termed 'finance sensitivity' since the crucial point is the cost of carry on an issue. In this sense, fluctuations in short term rates are actually very important. This point will become clearer in Chapter 7 where leveraging hedge investments is considered.

Figure 5.5 is replicated from an example of the five year plain vanilla convertible bond shown in Chapter 4, and shows the sensitivity of the bond to changes in interest rate levels.

Figure 5.6 considers the relative behaviour of a convertible bond to a straight bond equivalent. It not only considers a ten year bond, but also a one year and five year example of this ratio of rhos for a large range of share prices. When interpreting the graph, deep out of the money the rho ratio approaches 1 or 100%, signifying that the convert and straight bond equivalent have the same interest rate sensitivity.

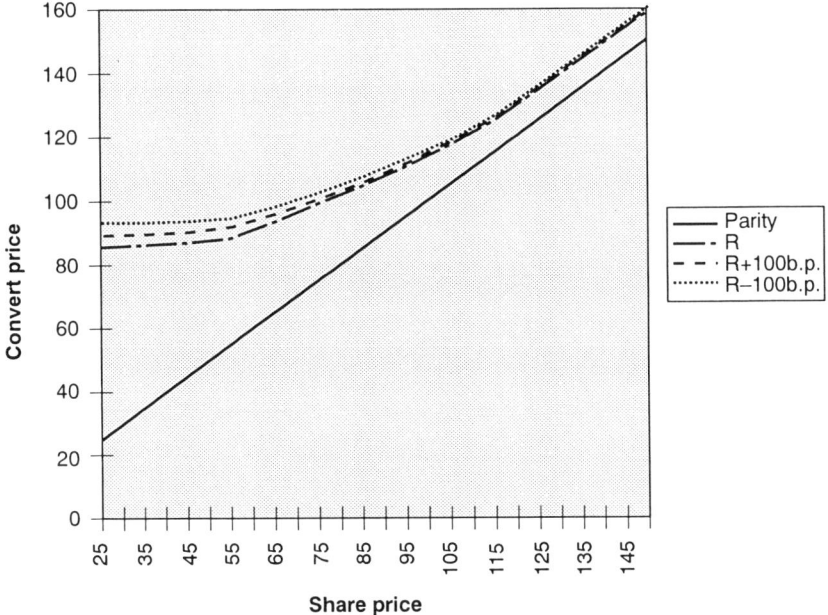

Figure 5.5: Impact of varying interest rates on convertible bonds

BOND FUTURES AND HEDGING INTEREST RATE RISK

Given the importance of interest rates when investing in convertible bonds, it is relevant for investors to at least be aware of the basic framework and nature of bond futures. The following is a relatively simple outline of the description of the *Treasury Bond Future Contract* and how it might be used to hedge interest rate risk. The Treasury Bond Future is the most popular long-term interest rate futures contract and is traded on the Chicago Board of Trade (CBOT).

On the first day of the delivery month, any government bond with more than fifteen years to maturity and not callable for more than fifteen years as well, may be delivered. Particularly active as well and in contrast are the *Treasury Note* and *5-year Treasury Note Futures contracts*. Delivery of the T-Note may take place in any note with maturity between six and a half years and ten years. Any of the four most recently auctioned T-notes may be delivered.

The following contains pertinent details of the 'Long Bond'. It is briefly shown how to interpret and arrive at the details :

Treasury Bond prices are quoted in dollars and 32nds of a dollar (Face value of US$100):

Cash price = Quoted price + Accrued interest since last coupon date   (5.6)

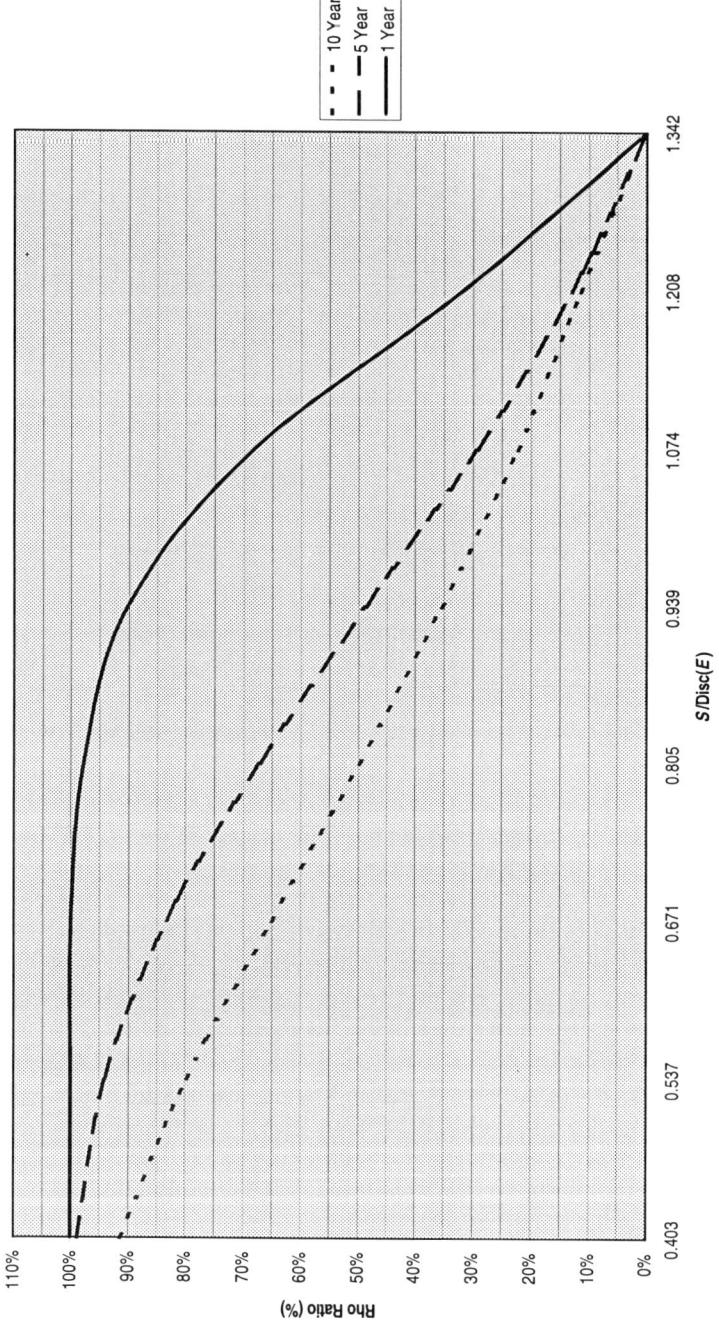

Figure 5.6: Rho relatives of typical convertible bonds

The Treasury Bond futures prices are quoted in the same way as the bond itself and delivery per contract is US$100,000 of face value of the bond.

The **Conversion factor** is important and may be defined as the price received by the party with the short position, e.g.:

Cash received by short = Quoted price × Conversion factor

+Accrued on the delivery bond   (5.7)

Quoted price   = 90-00
Conversion factor = 1.3800
Accrued interest   = US$3.00 per US$100 face value
Cash received   = US$127.2 per US$100

The conversion factor is equal to the value of the bond on the first day of the delivery month on the assumption that the interest rate for all maturities equals 8% p.a.

Example
Coupon = 10%
25 Years to maturity
Coupons paid semi-annually, 5% paid semi-annual
Discount rate is assumed 8%
For $I = 1–50$
Conversion factor = 1.2148

At any given time, there are about thirty bonds that can be delivered in the CBOT Treasury Bond futures contract. The party that is short can choose which is *cheapest to deliver*.

The cheapest to deliver bond will be that which has the least value of the following:

Cheapest to deliver = Quoted price

−(Quoted futures price × Conversion factor)   (5.8)

The following relationship outlines the theoretical futures price for the Treasury Bond contract if it is assumed that the delivery date and the cheapest to deliver bond are known:

$$F = (S - E)e^{r(T-t)} \qquad (5.9)$$

where F = the futures price
     S = the cash bond price
     T = maturity, t is the current time
     V = the present value of the coupons

ESTABLISHMENT OF AN INTEREST RATE HEDGE USING FUTURES

It is assumed that we have a straight bond portfolio worth US$10 million on 7 November 1994, with a duration of 7.2 years. It is further assumed that in this case the December Treasury Bond futures contract is used to hedge the value of the portfolio. The futures price is 96-07 (US$96,218.75). The cheapest to deliver bond is $9\frac{7}{8}\%$ 15 November 2011 with duration of 9.19.

The duration based hedge ratio is then equal to:

$$N^* = SD_s / FD_f \qquad (5.10)$$

or $(10,000,000/96,218.75) \times (7.2/9.19) = 81$ contracts.

This approximation makes the duration of the portfolio zero.

It is common in practice that short term rates are usually more volatile and may not always be correlated with long term rates. Non-parallel shifts are a real problem over longer time intervals when attempting to hedge out interest rate risk, but over small intervals of time, this assumption is a reasonable one.

Appendix: Price/Yield Relationships and Price Risk

Table 5A.1: One year straight bond

Years to Maturity		1	Cpn Freq		1
Today		Maturity	Redemption		100
09/Feb./96		08/Feb./97			

BOND PRICING MATRIX

Yield/ Coupon (%)	1.00%	2.00%	3.00%	4.00%	5.00%	6.00%	7.00%	8.00%	9.00%	10.00%
5.00	96.20	97.15	98.10	99.05	100.00	100.95	101.90	102.85	103.80	104.75
5.50	95.75	96.69	97.64	98.58	99.53	100.47	101.42	102.36	103.31	104.25
6.00	95.30	96.24	97.18	98.12	99.06	100.00	100.94	101.88	102.82	103.76
6.50	94.85	95.79	96.72	97.66	98.59	99.53	100.47	101.40	102.34	103.28
7.00	94.41	95.34	96.27	97.20	98.13	99.07	100.00	100.93	101.86	102.79
7.50	93.97	94.90	95.82	96.75	97.68	98.61	99.53	100.46	101.39	102.32
8.00	93.53	94.46	95.38	96.31	97.23	98.15	99.08	100.00	100.92	101.85
8.50	93.11	94.02	94.94	95.86	96.78	97.70	98.62	99.54	100.46	101.38
9.00	92.68	93.59	94.51	95.42	96.34	97.25	98.17	99.08	100.00	100.91
9.50	92.26	93.17	94.08	94.99	95.90	96.81	97.72	98.63	99.54	100.45
10.00	91.84	92.75	93.65	94.56	95.46	96.37	97.28	98.18	99.09	100.00
10.50	91.42	92.33	93.23	94.13	95.03	95.94	96.84	97.74	98.64	99.55
11.00	91.01	91.91	92.81	93.71	94.61	95.51	96.40	97.30	98.20	99.10
11.50	90.61	91.50	92.39	93.29	94.18	95.08	95.97	96.87	97.76	98.66
12.00	90.20	91.09	91.98	92.87	93.76	94.65	95.54	96.44	97.33	98.22
12.50	89.80	90.69	91.58	92.46	93.35	94.23	95.12	96.01	96.89	97.78
13.00	89.41	90.29	91.17	92.05	92.94	93.82	94.70	95.58	96.47	97.35
13.50	89.01	89.89	90.77	91.65	92.53	93.41	94.28	95.16	96.04	96.92
14.00	88.62	89.50	90.37	91.25	92.12	93.00	93.87	94.75	95.62	96.50
14.50	88.24	89.11	89.98	90.85	91.72	92.59	93.46	94.33	95.21	96.08
15.00	87.86	88.72	89.59	90.46	91.32	92.19	93.06	93.92	94.79	95.66

PRICE RISK MATRIX

Yield/ Coupon (%)	1.00%	2.00%	3.00%	4.00%	5.00%	6.00%	7.00%	8.00%	9.00%	10.00%
5.00										
5.50	0.45	0.46	0.46	0.47	0.47	0.48	0.48	0.48	0.49	0.49
6.00	0.45	0.45	0.46	0.46	0.47	0.47	0.47	0.48	0.48	0.49
6.50	0.44	0.45	0.45	0.46	0.46	0.47	0.47	0.47	0.48	0.48
7.00	0.44	0.44	0.45	0.45	0.46	0.46	0.47	0.47	0.47	0.48
7.50	0.44	0.44	0.44	0.45	0.45	0.46	0.46	0.47	0.47	0.47
8.00	0.43	0.44	0.44	0.44	0.45	0.45	0.46	0.46	0.47	0.47
8.50	0.43	0.43	0.44	0.44	0.44	0.45	0.45	0.46	0.46	0.47
9.00	0.42	0.43	0.43	0.44	0.44	0.45	0.45	0.45	0.46	0.46
9.50	0.42	0.42	0.43	0.43	0.44	0.44	0.45	0.45	0.45	0.46
10.00	0.42	0.42	0.42	0.43	0.43	0.44	0.44	0.45	0.45	0.45
10.50	0.41	0.42	0.42	0.42	0.43	0.43	0.44	0.44	0.45	0.45
11.00	0.41	0.41	0.42	0.42	0.43	0.43	0.43	0.44	0.44	0.45
11.50	0.41	0.41	0.41	0.42	0.42	0.43	0.43	0.43	0.44	0.44
12.00	0.40	0.41	0.41	0.41	0.42	0.42	0.43	0.43	0.43	0.44
12.50	0.40	0.40	0.41	0.41	0.41	0.42	0.42	0.43	0.43	0.43
13.00	0.39	0.40	0.40	0.41	0.41	0.41	0.42	0.42	0.43	0.43
13.50	0.39	0.40	0.40	0.40	0.41	0.41	0.41	0.42	0.42	0.43
14.00	0.39	0.39	0.40	0.40	0.40	0.41	0.41	0.41	0.42	0.42
14.50	0.38	0.39	0.39	0.40	0.40	0.40	0.41	0.41	0.41	0.42
15.00										

Table 5A.2: Five year straight bond

Years to Maturity		5	Cpn Freq		1
Today		Maturity	Redemption		100
09/Feb./96		08/Feb./01			

BOND PRICING MATRIX

Yield/ Coupon (%)	1.00%	2.00%	3.00%	4.00%	5.00%	6.00%	7.00%	8.00%	9.00%	10.00%
5.00	82.69	87.02	91.35	95.67	100.00	104.33	108.65	112.93	117.31	121.64
5.50	80.79	85.06	89.33	93.60	97.87	102.13	106.40	110.67	114.94	119.21
6.00	78.95	83.16	87.37	91.58	95.79	100.00	104.21	108.42	112.63	116.84
6.50	77.15	81.31	85.46	89.62	93.77	97.92	102.08	106.23	110.38	114.54
7.00	75.41	79.51	83.61	87.70	91.80	95.90	100.00	104.10	108.20	112.29
7.50	73.71	77.76	81.80	85.85	89.89	93.93	97.98	102.02	106.07	110.11
8.00	72.06	76.05	80.05	84.04	88.03	92.02	96.01	100.00	103.99	107.98
8.50	70.46	74.40	78.34	82.27	86.21	90.15	94.09	98.03	101.97	105.91
9.00	68.90	72.78	76.67	80.56	84.45	88.34	92.22	96.11	100.00	103.89
9.50	67.38	71.21	75.05	78.89	82.73	86.57	90.40	94.24	98.08	101.92
10.00	65.90	69.69	73.48	77.26	81.05	84.84	88.63	92.42	96.21	100.00
10.50	64.46	68.20	71.94	75.68	79.42	83.16	86.90	90.65	94.39	98.13
11.00	63.06	66.75	70.44	74.14	77.83	81.53	85.22	88.92	92.61	96.30
11.50	61.69	65.34	68.99	72.64	76.28	79.93	83.58	87.23	90.88	94.53
12.00	60.36	63.97	67.57	71.17	74.78	78.38	81.98	85.59	89.19	92.79
12.50	59.07	62.63	66.19	69.75	73.31	76.86	80.42	83.98	87.54	91.10
13.00	57.81	61.33	64.84	68.36	71.87	75.39	78.90	82.42	85.94	89.45
13.50	56.58	60.06	63.53	67.00	70.48	73.95	77.42	80.90	84.37	87.84
14.00	55.39	58.82	62.25	65.68	69.11	72.55	75.98	79.41	82.84	86.27
14.50	54.22	57.61	61.00	64.39	67.79	71.18	74.57	77.96	81.35	84.74
15.00	53.09	56.44	59.79	63.14	66.49	69.84	73.19	76.54	79.89	83.24

PRICE RISK MATRIX

Yield/ Coupon (%)	1.00%	2.00%	3.00%	4.00%	5.00%	6.00%	7.00%	8.00%	9.00%	10.00%
5.00										
5.50	1.87	1.93	1.99	2.05	2.11	2.16	2.22	2.28	2.34	2.40
6.00	1.82	1.88	1.93	1.99	2.05	2.11	2.16	2.22	2.28	2.33
6.50	1.77	1.83	1.88	1.94	1.99	2.05	2.11	2.16	2.22	2.27
7.00	1.72	1.78	1.83	1.88	1.94	1.99	2.05	2.10	2.16	2.21
7.50	1.67	1.73	1.78	1.83	1.89	1.94	2.00	2.05	2.10	2.16
8.00	1.63	1.68	1.73	1.79	1.84	1.89	1.94	2.00	2.05	2.10
8.50	1.58	1.64	1.69	1.74	1.79	1.84	1.89	1.94	2.00	2.05
9.00	1.54	1.59	1.64	1.69	1.74	1.79	1.84	1.89	1.94	1.99
9.50	1.50	1.55	1.60	1.65	1.70	1.75	1.80	1.85	1.89	1.94
10.00	1.46	1.51	1.56	1.60	1.65	1.70	1.75	1.80	1.85	1.89
10.50	1.42	1.47	1.52	1.56	1.61	1.66	1.70	1.75	1.80	1.85
11.00	1.38	1.43	1.48	1.52	1.57	1.62	1.66	1.71	1.75	1.80
11.50	1.35	1.39	1.44	1.48	1.53	1.57	1.62	1.67	1.71	1.76
12.00	1.31	1.36	1.40	1.44	1.49	1.53	1.58	1.62	1.67	1.71
12.50	1.28	1.32	1.36	1.41	1.45	1.50	1.54	1.58	1.63	1.67
13.00	1.24	1.29	1.33	1.37	1.42	1.46	1.50	1.54	1.59	1.63
13.50	1.21	1.25	1.30	1.34	1.38	1.42	1.46	1.51	1.55	1.59
14.00	1.18	1.22	1.26	1.30	1.35	1.39	1.43	1.47	1.51	1.55
14.50	1.15	1.19	1.23	1.27	1.31	1.35	1.39	1.43	1.47	1.51

Table 5A.3: Ten year straight bond

Years to Maturity		10	Cpn Freq		1
Today		Maturity	Redemption		100
09/Feb./96		08/Feb./06			

BOND PRICING MATRIX

Yield/ Coupon (%)	1.00%	2.00%	3.00%	4.00%	5.00%	6.00%	7.00%	8.00%	9.00%	10.00%
5.00	69.12	76.84	84.56	92.28	100.00	107.72	115.44	123.16	130.88	138.60
5.50	66.09	73.62	81.16	88.70	96.23	103.77	111.30	118.84	126.38	133.91
6.00	63.21	70.57	77.92	85.28	92.64	100.00	107.36	114.72	122.08	129.43
6.50	60.47	67.66	74.84	82.03	89.22	96.41	103.59	110.78	117.97	125.16
7.00	57.87	64.89	71.91	78.93	85.96	92.98	100.00	107.02	114.04	121.07
7.50	55.39	62.25	69.12	75.98	82.84	89.71	96.57	103.43	110.29	117.16
8.00	53.04	59.75	66.46	73.16	79.87	86.58	93.29	100.00	106.71	113.42
8.50	50.80	57.36	63.92	70.48	77.04	83.60	90.16	96.72	103.28	109.84
9.00	48.67	55.08	61.50	67.92	74.33	80.75	87.17	93.58	100.00	106.42
9.50	46.64	52.92	59.19	65.47	71.75	78.03	84.30	90.58	96.86	103.14
10.00	44.71	50.85	56.99	63.14	69.28	75.43	81.57	87.71	93.86	100.00
10.50	42.87	48.88	54.90	60.91	66.92	72.94	78.95	84.96	90.98	96.99
11.00	41.12	47.00	52.89	58.78	64.67	70.56	76.45	82.33	88.22	94.11
11.50	39.45	45.21	50.98	56.75	62.51	68.28	74.05	79.81	85.58	91.35
12.00	37.86	43.51	49.16	54.80	60.45	66.10	71.75	77.40	83.05	88.70
12.50	36.34	41.88	47.41	52.95	58.48	64.02	69.55	75.09	80.62	86.16
13.00	34.89	40.32	45.74	51.17	56.60	62.02	67.45	72.87	78.30	83.72
13.50	33.52	38.83	44.15	49.47	54.79	60.11	65.43	70.75	76.06	81.38
14.00	32.20	37.41	42.63	47.85	53.06	58.28	63.49	68.71	73.92	79.14
14.50	30.94	36.06	41.17	46.29	51.40	56.52	61.63	66.75	71.86	76.98
15.00	29.75	34.76	39.78	44.80	49.82	54.84	59.85	64.87	69.89	74.91

PRICE RISK MATRIX

Yield/ Coupon (%)	1.00%	2.00%	3.00%	4.00%	5.00%	6.00%	7.00%	8.00%	9.00%	10.00%
5.00										
5.50	2.56	3.14	3.32	3.50	3.68	3.86	4.04	4.22	4.40	4.58
6.00	2.81	2.98	3.16	3.33	3.51	3.68	3.86	4.03	4.20	4.38
6.50	2.67	2.84	3.01	3.17	3.34	3.51	3.68	3.85	4.02	4.18
7.00	2.54	2.70	2.86	3.03	3.19	3.35	3.51	3.67	3.84	4.00
7.50	2.41	2.57	2.73	2.88	3.04	3.20	3.35	3.51	3.67	3.82
8.00	2.30	2.45	2.60	2.75	2.90	3.05	3.20	3.36	3.51	3.66
8.50	2.19	2.33	2.48	2.62	2.77	2.92	3.06	3.21	3.35	3.50
9.00	2.08	2.22	2.36	2.50	2.64	2.79	2.93	3.07	3.21	3.35
9.50	1.98	2.12	2.25	2.39	2.53	2.66	2.80	2.94	3.07	3.21
10.00	1.89	2.02	2.15	2.28	2.41	2.55	2.68	2.81	2.94	3.07
10.50	1.80	1.92	2.05	2.18	2.31	2.43	2.56	2.69	2.82	2.84
11.00	1.71	1.83	1.96	2.08	2.20	2.33	2.45	2.57	2.70	2.82
11.50	1.63	1.75	1.87	1.99	2.11	2.23	2.35	2.47	2.59	2.71
12.00	1.55	1.67	1.78	1.90	2.02	2.13	2.25	2.36	2.48	2.59
12.50	1.48	1.59	1.71	1.82	1.93	2.04	2.15	2.26	2.38	2.49
13.00	1.41	1.52	1.63	1.74	1.85	1.95	2.05	2.17	2.28	2.39
13.50	1.35	1.45	1.56	1.66	1.77	1.87	1.98	2.08	2.19	2.29
14.00	1.29	1.39	1.49	1.59	1.69	1.79	1.90	2.00	2.10	2.20
14.50	1.23	1.33	1.42	1.52	1.62	1.72	1.82	1.92	2.02	2.11

Table 5A.4: Twenty year straight bond

Years to Maturity		20	Cpn Freq		1
Today		Maturity	Redemption		100
09/Feb./96		08/Feb./16			

BOND PRICING MATRIX

Yield/ Coupon (%)	1.00%	2.00%	3.00%	4.00%	5.00%	6.00%	7.00%	8.00%	9.00%	10.00%
5.00	50.15	62.61	75.08	87.54	100.00	112.46	124.92	137.39	149.85	162.31
5.50	46.22	58.17	70.12	82.07	94.02	105.98	117.93	129.88	141.83	153.78
6.00	42.65	54.12	65.59	77.06	88.53	100.00	111.47	122.94	134.41	145.88
6.50	39.40	50.42	61.44	72.45	83.47	94.49	105.51	116.53	127.55	138.56
7.00	36.44	47.03	57.62	68.22	78.81	89.41	100.00	110.59	121.19	131.78
7.50	33.74	43.93	54.12	64.32	74.51	84.71	94.90	105.10	115.29	125.49
8.00	31.27	41.09	50.91	60.73	70.55	80.36	90.18	100.00	109.82	119.64
8.50	29.02	38.49	47.95	57.41	66.88	76.34	85.80	95.27	104.73	114.20
9.00	26.97	36.10	45.23	54.36	63.49	72.61	81.74	90.87	100.00	109.13
9.50	25.09	33.91	42.72	51.53	60.34	69.16	77.97	86.78	95.59	104.41
10.00	23.38	31.89	40.41	48.92	57.43	65.95	74.46	82.97	91.49	100.00
10.50	21.81	30.04	38.27	46.50	54.73	62.96	71.19	79.42	87.65	95.88
11.00	20.37	28.33	36.29	44.26	52.22	60.18	68.15	76.11	84.07	92.04
11.50	19.05	26.76	34.47	42.18	49.89	57.60	65.31	73.02	80.73	88.44
12.00	17.84	25.31	32.78	40.24	47.71	55.18	62.65	70.12	77.59	85.06
12.50	16.72	23.97	31.21	38.45	45.69	52.93	60.17	67.41	74.66	81.90
13.00	15.70	22.73	29.75	36.78	43.80	50.83	57.85	64.88	71.90	78.93
13.50	14.76	21.58	28.40	35.22	42.04	48.86	55.68	62.50	69.31	76.13
14.00	13.90	20.52	27.15	33.77	40.39	47.01	53.64	60.26	66.88	73.51
14.50	13.10	19.54	25.98	32.41	38.85	45.29	51.72	58.16	64.60	71.03
15.00	12.37	18.63	24.89	31.15	37.41	43.67	49.93	56.18	62.44	68.70

PRICE RISK MATRIX

Yield/ Coupon (%)	1.00%	2.00%	3.00%	4.00%	5.00%	6.00%	7.00%	8.00%	9.00%	10.00%
5.00	3.75	4.25	4.74	5.24	5.73	6.23	6.73	7.22	7.72	8.22
5.50	3.41	3.88	4.34	4.81	5.28	5.74	6.21	6.67	7.14	7.61
6.00	3.11	3.55	3.98	4.42	4.86	5.30	5.73	6.17	6.61	7.05
6.50	2.83	3.24	3.66	4.07	4.48	4.89	5.30	5.72	6.13	6.54
7.00	2.58	2.97	3.36	3.75	4.13	4.52	4.91	5.30	5.68	6.07
7.50	2.36	2.72	3.09	3.45	3.82	4.18	4.55	4.91	5.28	5.65
8.00	2.15	2.50	2.84	3.19	3.53	3.87	4.22	4.56	4.91	5.25
8.50	1.97	2.29	2.62	2.94	3.27	3.59	3.92	4.24	4.57	4.89
9.00	1.80	2.10	2.41	2.72	3.03	3.33	3.64	3.95	4.26	4.56
9.50	1.64	1.93	2.23	2.52	2.81	3.10	3.39	3.68	3.97	4.26
10.00	1.51	1.78	2.06	2.33	2.61	2.88	3.16	3.43	3.71	3.98
10.50	1.38	1.64	1.90	2.16	2.42	2.68	2.94	3.20	3.46	3.72
11.00	1.27	1.51	1.76	2.01	2.25	2.50	2.75	2.99	3.24	3.49
11.50	1.16	1.40	1.63	1.86	2.10	2.33	2.57	2.80	3.04	3.27
12.00	1.07	1.29	1.51	1.73	1.96	2.18	2.40	2.62	2.85	3.07
12.50	0.98	1.19	1.40	1.61	1.83	2.04	2.25	2.46	2.67	2.88
13.00	0.90	1.10	1.30	1.50	1.71	1.91	2.11	2.31	2.51	2.71
13.50	0.83	1.02	1.21	1.40	1.59	1.79	1.98	2.17	2.36	2.55
14.00	0.76	0.95	1.13	1.31	1.49	1.67	1.86	2.04	2.22	2.40

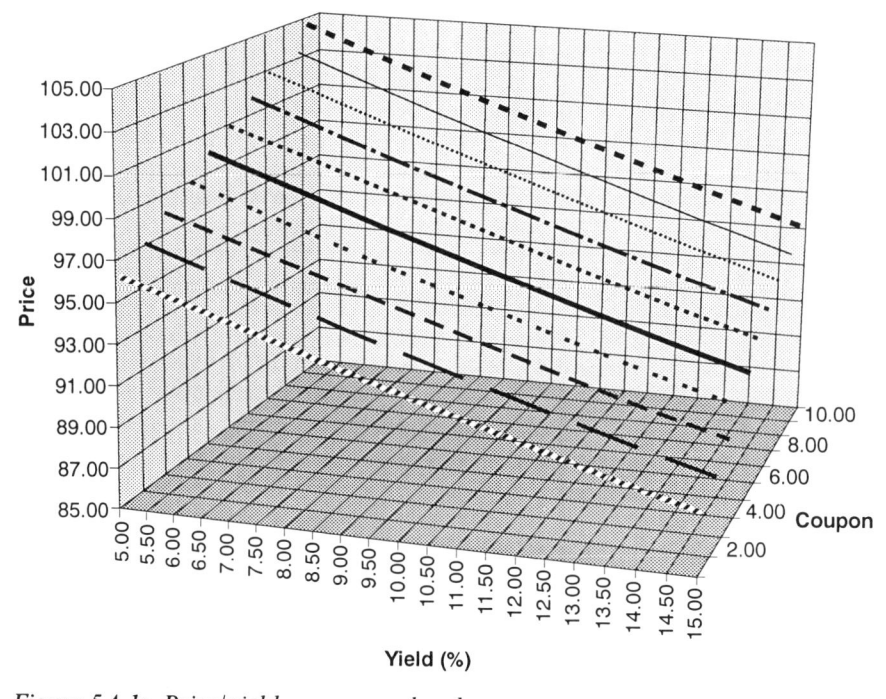

Figure 5A.1: Price/yield – one year bond

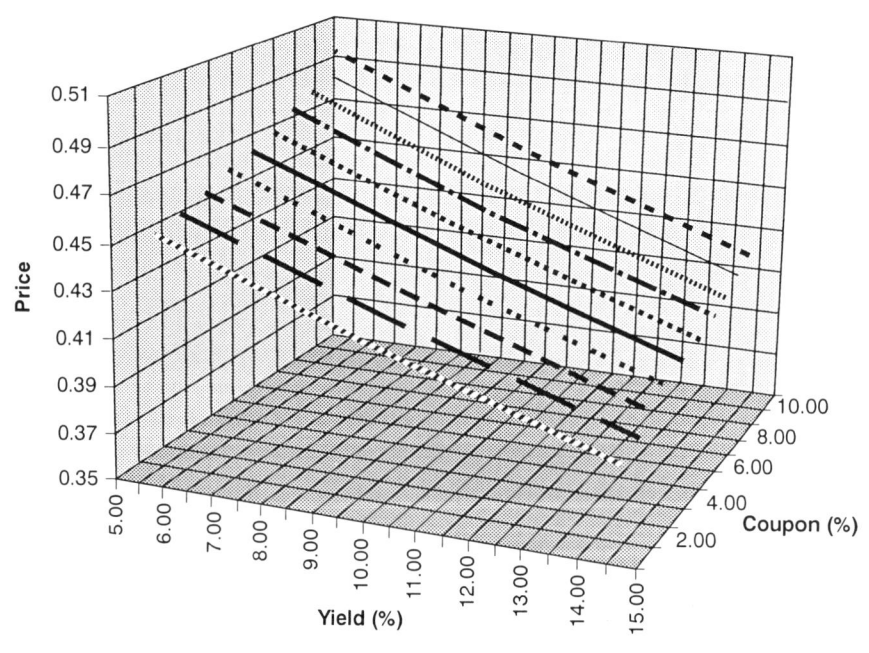

Figure 5A.2: dP/dY – one year bond

82

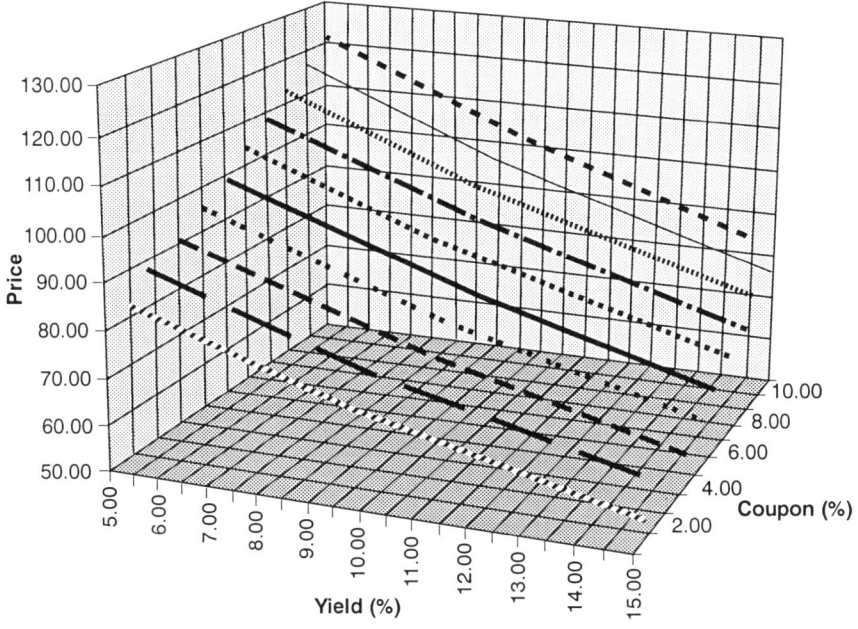

Figure 5A.3: Price/yield – five year bond

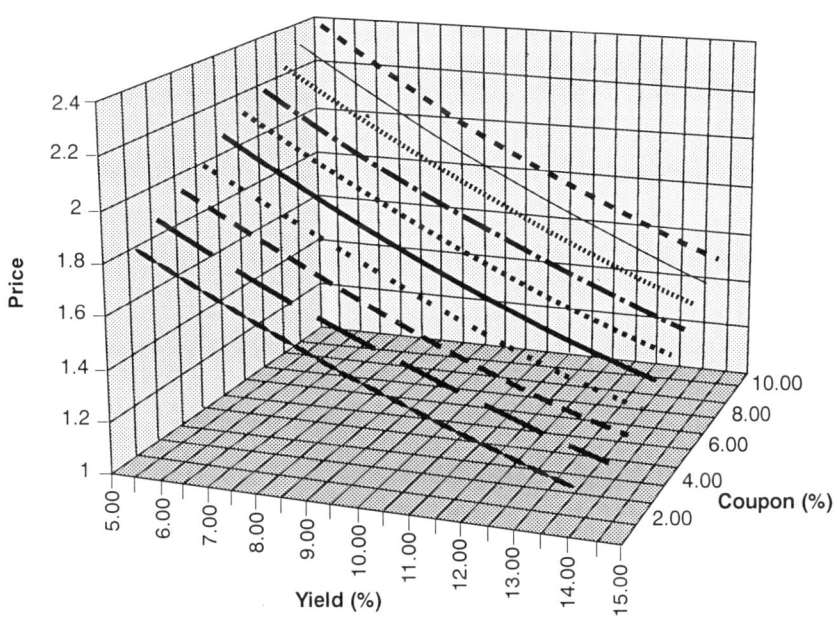

Figure 5A.4: dP/dY – five year bond

83

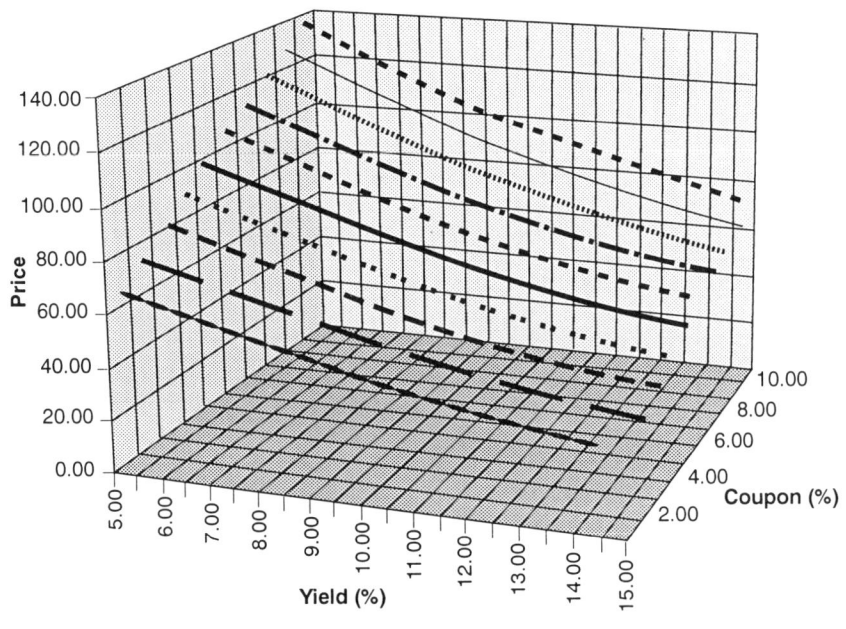

Figure 5A.5: Price/yield – ten year bond

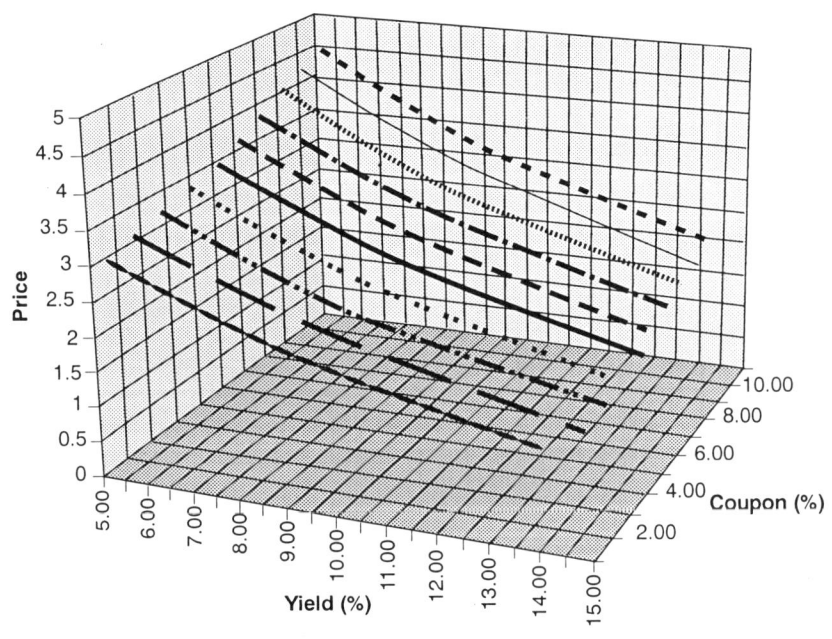

Figure 5A.6: dP/dY – ten year bond

84

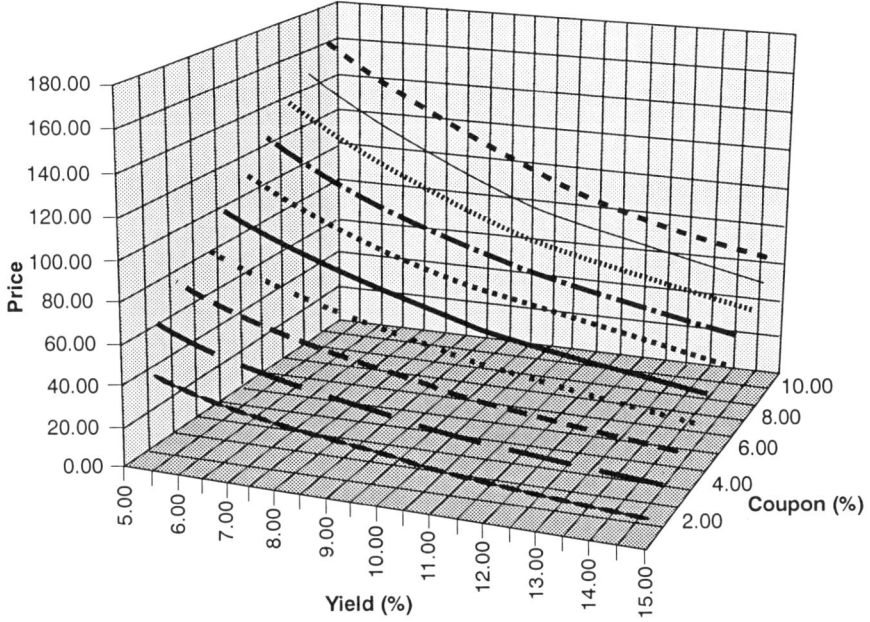

Figure 5A.7: Price/yield – twenty year bond

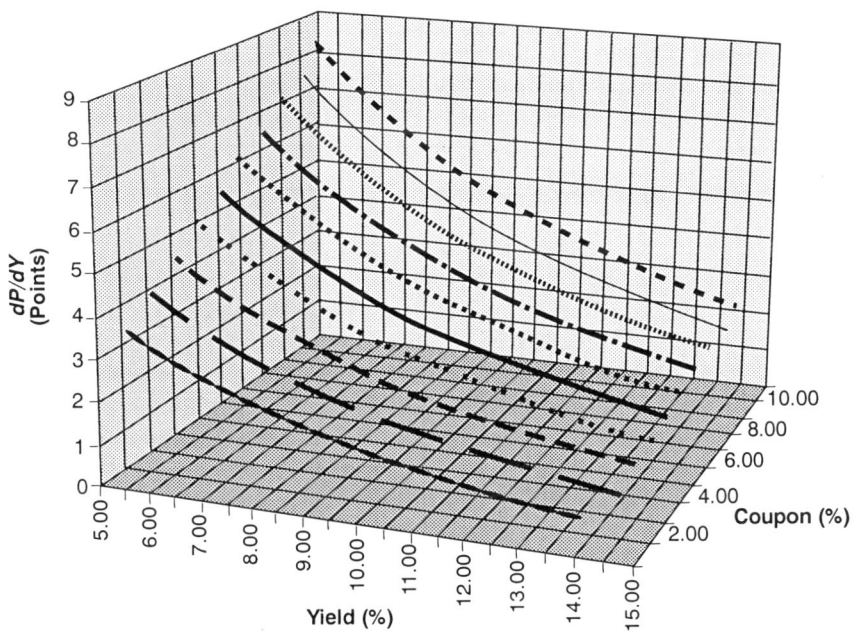

Figure 5A.8: dP/dY – twenty year bond

85

6: Default Risk Assessed

One of the things which makes the analysis of convertible bonds more difficult relates to the whole question of default risk inherent in the instruments. Strictly, shares do not have default risk – *they do not promise a particular set of cash flows in the future.* This chapter is devoted to a more systematic assessment of this subject area, and once we have established by whom and how ratings are established for companies, and what exactly is meant by 'default risk', we specifically attempt to pinpoint how an approach may be taken to value this element of a convertible bond price.

'Default' specifically points to the failure on the part of a corporation to meet a contractual payment obligation, i.e. missing or delaying the payment of interest and/or redemption proceeds, 'Distressed exchanges' point to circumstances where holders of debt are offered financial securities of less commitment, such as lower coupons or redemption proceeds. Other companies deliberately make payment in default but within a given period permitted in the indenture of the bond.

ROLE OF THE RATING AGENCIES

There are considerable numbers of credit rating agencies. By far the most well known are Standard and Poors (S&P) and Moody's Investors Service. In certain countries, many companies are not assessed by these agencies, or there may be more specialised agencies. For example, Mikunis, Japan Bond Rating Agency, and JCR are well known in Japan. One of the fastest growth areas for convertible bonds in recent years has been from newly developed 'Tigers' of the Far East where assessment of the credit worthiness of corporations is particularly difficult. This chapter aims to help in this process.

'Letters' are usually assigned to companies to help investors draw conclusions regarding credit worthiness at a glance. Table 6.1 provides examples of letters assigned by S&P and Moody's.

The top four ratings by both credit agencies are regarded as *investment grade*. Others are *speculative grade*. A company which has seen its standing fall

Table 6.1: Ratings of Standard & Poors/Moody's

S & P	Moodys	
AAA	**Aaa** ⎫	*Investment Grade* – These top four grades represent an
AA	**Aa** ⎪	ability to repay promised future payments on the part of the
A	**A** ⎬	borrower, ranging from excellent ('gilt edged'), to strong but
BBB	**Baa** ⎭	with certain speculative elements
BB	**Ba** ⎫	*Speculative Grade* – These grades are also termed '*junk* debt',
B	**B** ⎪	ranging from least speculative (**BB/Ba**) to most speculative
CCC	**Caa** ⎬	Standard & Poors have two further categories in the form of **CI**
CC	**Ca** ⎪	(bonds where interest is no longer being paid) and **D** which
C	**C** ⎭	represents bonds where payment is in default

from investment to speculative grade is known as a *'fallen angel'*, and speculative grades are also referred to as *'junk'*.

When considering the rating of companies, the credit agencies will tend to look upon them more kindly if their debt/equity ratio is lower (less leveraged), there is an adequate asset base, and earnings per share is not very volatile. Furthermore, they will be concerned with the level of subordination of debt. However, the agencies will not only rely on past financial data, but will make an effort to combine both statistical and non-statistical data to project forwards.

DEFAULT PREMIUMS

Figure 6.1 shows a number of key features relating to the pricing of a corporate bond.

The bond under consideration has a promised yield to maturity of 10%. The expected yield to maturity is shown as 8% and the yield to maturity of a default free bond which is used as a benchmark is 7%. Now there are a number of

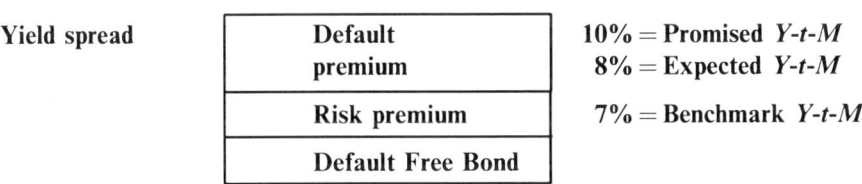

Yield spread	**Default premium**	10% = **Promised** *Y-t-M*
		8% = **Expected** *Y-t-M*
	Risk premium	7% = **Benchmark** *Y-t-M*
	Default Free Bond	

Figure 6.1: Default premiums

reasons why promised and actual yields to maturity may differ, one of which relates to default risk. It is also important to understand what is meant by the risk and default premium elements of the pricing respectively.

If default of one company was completely unrelated to default of others, then one would anticipate that the expected return to a portfolio of corporate bonds would equal that of the default free bond, all other things being equal, because with a very well diversified portfolio, gains from companies which do not default should offset losses from cases of default. One can therefore see why a default premium exists in Figure 6.1 However, let us see why risk premium exists. This relates to *systematic* or *non-diversifiable risk*. In other words, experience tells us that it is during more severe recessions that there are more defaults. This non-diversifiable risk merits the risk premium.

This raises an interesting point. The rating agencies assignments are *relative* not absolute. This is confirmed by comparing yields of different rated bonds in Figure 6.2. The yield spreads differ over time.

Edward Altman's maturity tables are reproduced in Table 6.2. The bonds are considered over the period 1971–90, and given an initial rating, default experience is examined. The findings for AA rated bonds appears rather odd, but otherwise it is clearly shown that the cumulative rate of default increases with time.

In fact, during the early 1990s we witnessed the highest levels of default since the Second World War. In 1990, Moodys reported that a total of 97 public corporations world-wide defaulted on the equivalent of US$22 billion of debt. In 1991, the same respective statistics were 99 public corporations and US$20 billion of debt. However, by 1994, although still high, the level of defaults had fallen the equivalent of US$2.3 billion of debt from 24 public corporations.

A study of Table 6.3 is interesting, a summary of defaulted bond price distributions, reproduced from *Probability of Default: A Derivatives Perspective*, by Fons and Carty of Moody's Investors Service.

The authors considered defaulting bonds over the period 1 January 1974 to 1 January 1995. The findings are as one would expect, with more senior ranked holders of debt having priority over more junior debtholders. Senior secured holders of defaulting companies received US$ 53.11 of the par amount on average, with senior unsecured and subordinated holders receiving US$49.86 and US$32.83, respectively, on average.

Also not surprisingly, the average defaulted bond price is a function of the level of gross domestic product (GDP) growth. However, note that the relatively high level of dispersion about the mean suggests a high degree of uncertainty.

Mathematical work is increasingly being applied to the question of default risk and credit spread analysis. For those who wish to read further on the subject, Cox *et al.* use a convenient framework, first used by Robert Merton in *On Corporate Debt* to analyse default premium rigorously and show that it

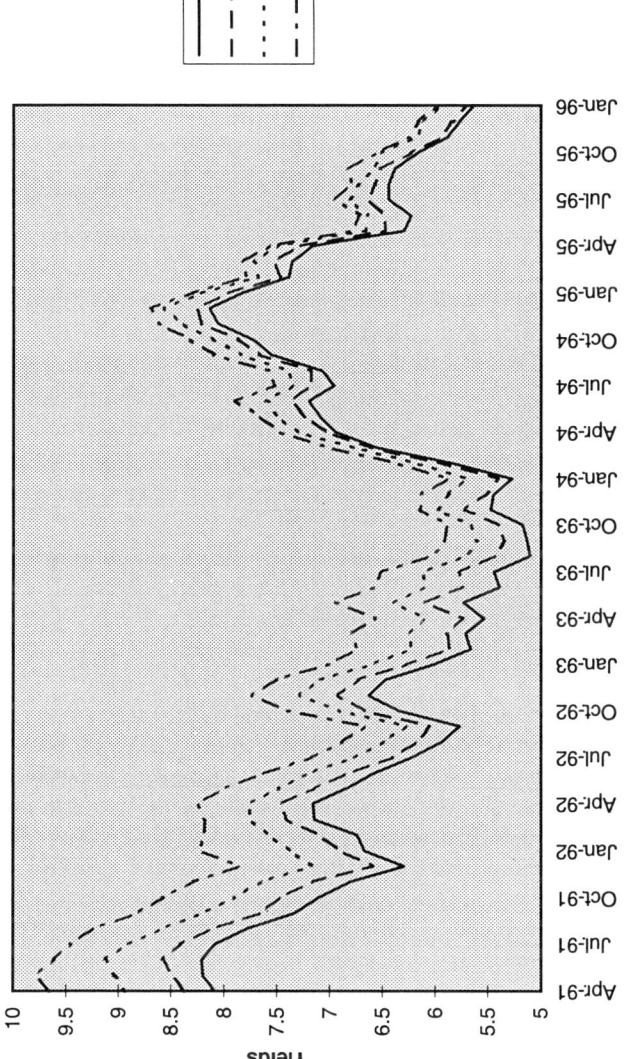

Figure 6.2: Bond yields by ratings, April 1991–January 1996

Table 6.2: Default rates, 1971–90

Years	AAA	AA	A	BBB	BB	B	CCC
1	0.00	0.00	0.00	0.03	0.00	0.87	1.31
2	0.00	0.00	0.30	0.57	0.93	3.22	4.00
3	0.00	1.11	0.60	0.85	1.36	9.41	19.72
4	0.00	1.42	0.65	1.34	3.98	16.37	36.67
5	0.00	1.70	0.65	1.54	5.93	20.87	38.08
6	0.14	1.70	0.73	1.81	7.38	26.48	40.58
7	0.19	1.91	0.87	2.70	10.91	29.62	–
8	0.19	1.93	0.94	2.83	10.91	31.74	–
9	0.19	2.01	1.28	2.99	10.91	39.38	–
10	0.19	2.11	1.28	3.85	13.86	40.86	–

Table 6.3: Summary of defaulted bond price distributions, 1974–95

Seniority	Average	Median	Std dev.	10th perc.	90th perc.
Senior secured	53.11	56.00	24.27	18.50	85.32
Senior insecured	49.86	46.56	26.32	11.46	87.88
Subordinated	32.83	30.17	19.67	9.18	60.40

'depends solely on capital structure, operating risk and debt maturity'. 'Capital structure' refers here to the debt/equity ratio (w), operating risk may be thought of as the volatility of the value of the firm (σ_v):

$$\textbf{Default premium} = f(w,\ \sigma_v, T) \tag{6.1}$$

The relationship with w and σ_v is always positive, but the relationship with time is complicated. Researchers have most often found an upward sloping term structure of credit risk for higher credit quality debt and a downward sloping term structure of credit risk for lower credit quality debt. A useful explanation for this is what has come to be known the 'Crisis at maturity theory'. That is, for companies which are viewed as speculative, there may be investor concern over the fact that the bulk of promised cash flows are more imminent.

CONVERTIBLE BONDS AND DEFAULT PREMIUMS

A required input into the binomial model presented in Chapter 4 is a credit adjusted interest rate. This is problematic in some cases. How do we know what theoretical spread to assume? There are a number of approaches which may be taken.

STRAIGHT BOND EQUIVALENT

Most obviously, the task is greatly eased if there is a straight bond equivalent from the corporate entity concerned, with similar coupon and maturity. One is likely to have to incorporate the fact that the convertible debt is subordinated. This procedure is not particularly difficult, but it should be apparent that very often the convertible security has been issued in lieu of a straight bond for a whole host of reasons. One could of course look for straight bonds of companies very similar in capital structure, and operating risk. These companies may well be in the same industrial sector. In practice, this often works well.

Increasingly, there is a well established swap market for the fixed income component of convertible bonds. Particularly for names with better ratings, those in the market will be very familiar with how much the bond should trade over the swap curve. For issues with lesser credit ratings, there will be bids for bonds reflecting a given spread over the swap curve, and typically those bidding will have an 'in-house' view on the credit worthiness of the issuer, which may be reinforced by the fact that they are existing shareholders in the company.

IMPLIED SPREAD

Credit rating agencies, as already mentioned, may not assign ratings at all to many companies with outstanding convertible debt, but we may still want to evaluate them. Many convertibles which are deep out of the money will have very little, or no option value. If, for example, an issue is 70% out of the money with two years to maturity, it will likely trade just like a straight bond, and therefore one can view the theoretical spread directly. On the other hand, what might be more sensible is to assume the price of the convert is 'fair', use the historic volatility and solve for the implied spread on a bond. This is not such a bad practice as one would imagine, given that as those with options experience will already know, deep out of the money instruments have a tendency to be more fairly or overpriced. Having completed this exercise, it may be helpful in assessing other issues from the same company which are more interesting. This might also prove useful when assessing companies which are rated very similarly.

SENSITIVITY TO CHANGES IN THEORETICAL SPREADS

Table 6.4 is reproduced from *Investments* by Sharpe *et al.*, and considers three groups of bond investments by Keystone, B1 through B4, the latter

91

Table 6.4: Risk/return on Keystone funds, 1968–91

	B1 Conservative	B2 Investment	B4 Discount
Annual return (% p.a.)	7.84	8.53	8.64
Std. dev. (% p.a.)	8.2	9.35	13.68
Beta value, relative to S & P 500	0.26	0.38	0.54
Proportion of variance, explained by S & P 500	0.28	0.45	0.42

representing the lowest rated bonds. As one would expect, B4 had the highest average annual return, but also the highest standard deviation.

It is interesting to see the extent to which the lowest rated bonds moved with equity. It is during periods of extreme volatility of the underlying equity market and distress in particular that theoretical spreads may widen drastically. The rate of change of the convertible with respect to the rate of change of the theoretical spread (TS) will be termed *omicron*:

$$\textbf{Omicron} = \frac{\delta CB}{\delta TS} \tag{6.2}$$

The sensitivity shown in Figure 6.3 is similar to the way we looked at other sensitivity measures in Chapter 4. For sake of clarity, the graph plots the theoretical price profile of a five year 1.5 % (semi-annual) convert with varying credit or theoretical spreads assumed. The riskless interest rate was assumed at 1.5%, volatility of 20%. CB is a convert which has a credit adjusted spread of 350 basis points over the curve, CB1 plots the profile for a bond 50 basis points over, and CB2 plots the bond 650 basis points over, the curve. We know that deeper in the money, default risk becomes less important and at the limit where we are hedged 'one for one', the risk free rate becomes the relevant rate: changing spreads have less impact on the price of a bond, the deeper it moves in the money. However, deep out of the money as the hedge ratio approaches zero, the credit adjusted spread changing has an increasing impact on the bond.

This in fact is confirmed by plotting changes in the bond price with respect to changes in the spread, as shown in Figure 6.4.

Spreads can be extremely dynamic. Considerable speculation can cause spreads to widen and close several hundred basis points in a very short period indeed. This kind of behaviour has been quite dramatic in cases such as *Eurodisney, Fokker*, or *Polly Peck*, for example, where public announcements caused substantial price swings. For this reason, the lower end of the price range for convertibles and bonds may be considered to be 'discontinuous'. The implications of this are considerable. For example, at the lower end of the delta function, if the convertible has not been swapped out, the hedge ratio may be

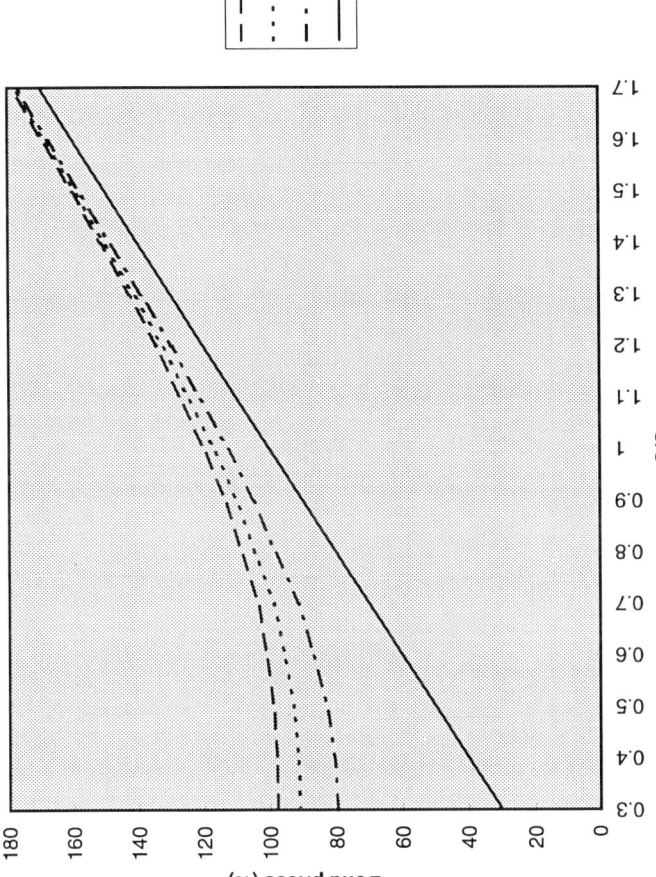

Figure 6.3: Impact of varying credit spreads

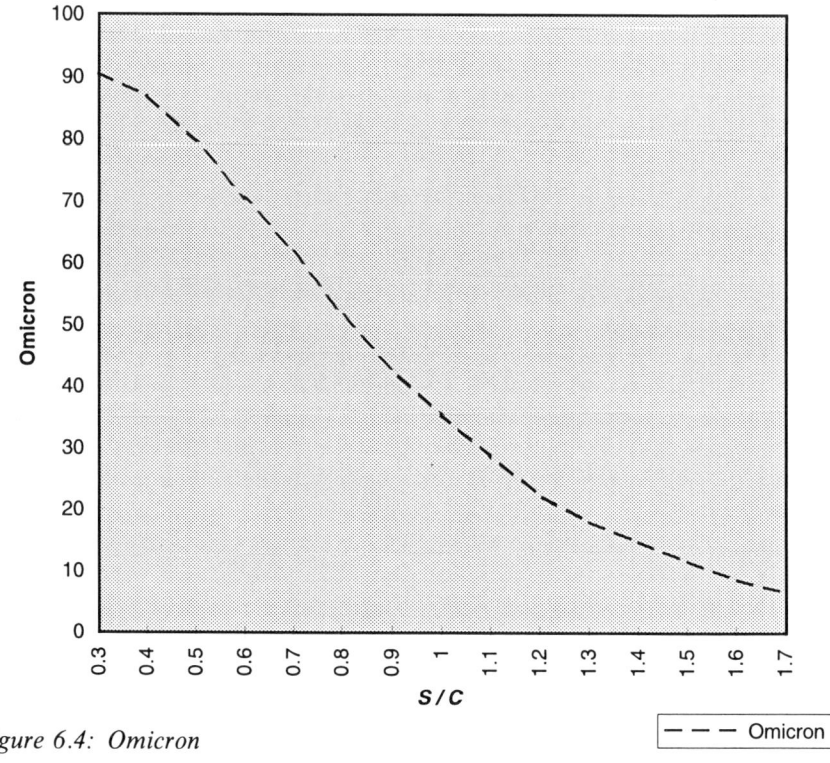

Figure 6.4: Omicron

$$- - -\ \text{Omicron}$$

greater than 100%. On a similar basis, in 1994, for example, many hedge funds long of converts in Hong Kong found that they were losing disproportionately. Share prices were falling and exhibiting extreme volatility and many funds were buying to lighten hedge ratios, but the fact is that spreads were simultaneously widening, thus completely negating the impact of share price declines.

7: Long Volatility

INTRODUCTION

Investors are used to the term 'long'. They may be long shares, long bonds or long index futures, in the sense that they have purchased them. But it is rather more difficult to grasp the concept of what it really means to be long of volatility, since it is intangible. This is the subject matter of the next section. In this chapter we address the course of action which is taken by a large group of investors globally to take advantage of opportunities when convertibles do not trade at a 'fair' level.

'Hedging' has been a term much abused over the years. It is used to describe many kinds of investors with differing risk perspectives. It certainly refers to being simultaneously long and short. Some hedgers may be long of an individual derivative and short the underlying security, while others may be short of a completely different security, such as an index future. Others may be leveraged and others may be not. Here we consider 'market neutral' *univariate market neutral hedging*, i.e. long on a convertible bond versus a short position in the underlying security.

We will first study the calculation of volatility, what it means and then consider problems and practical issues needed to value and trade convertibles. We will then be in a position to consider the establishment of hedge positions and simulations. This will give us an opportunity to focus specifically on the risks inherent in such strategies. Most importantly, and never addressed in books on the subject, what approach should be taken when these derivatives not only trade well below fair value, but actually become even cheaper?

WHAT IS MEANT BY 'VOLATILITY'?

The term 'volatility' is ubiquitous in option theory. It is a measure of risk and is most commonly denoted as σ. It is not easily observable like prices themselves. We know that there is a positive relationship between volatility of the underlying share and the value of the convertible bond. The more risky the

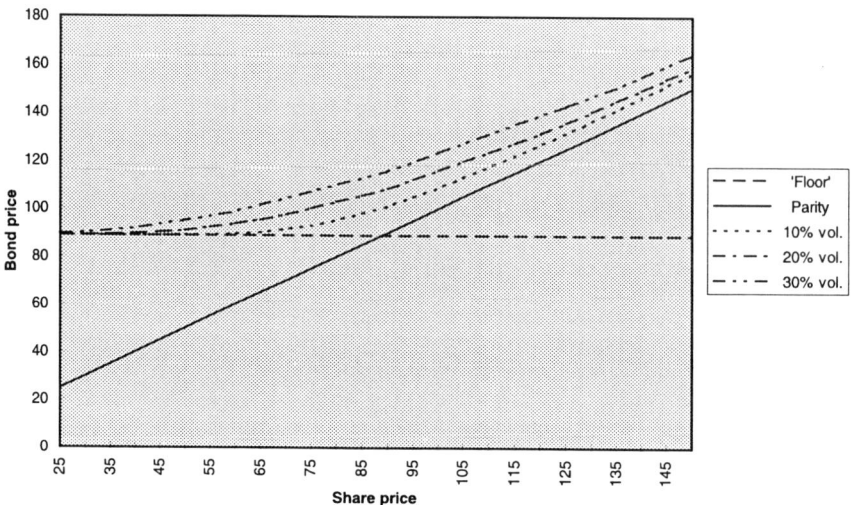

Figure 7.1: Varying volatility and the fair price of a convertible bond

underlying share, the more valuable the convertible becomes. We saw the impact of varying volatility on the fair price of the convert in Chapter 4. This is replicated in Figure 7.1.

In this chapter we will see why the convertible should be more valuable if the volatility of the underlying share is greater. Before measuring volatility, we first consider what are referred to as the '*returns*' to the underlying equity.

Returns are measured by *price relatives*. That is,

$$r_t = S_t/S_{t-1} \tag{7.1}$$

where r_t = share price relative in the present period
$\quad\quad S_t$ = current share price
and S_{t-1} = share price in the last time period

One actually considers the natural logarithm of the share price relatives so that returns are symmetrical. For example, if a share price rises from US$1.0 to US$1.1, the percentage gain is $+10\%$. If it then declines to US$1.0 again, the percentage decline is -9.909%. If we took logs, the price relative would have been 0.0953 in both cases:

$$R_t = \log(S_t/S_{t-1}) \tag{7.2}$$

To estimate volatility of the underlying share we calculate returns using daily, weekly, or monthly data. Weekly data works well in practice, for convertible bonds.

Table 7.1 lists share prices for Microsoft using weekly data and takes us through the estimation of volatility step by step.

Column (1) (*St*) is simply the daily share price at the close of business. *Column (2)* (*Rt*) lists the daily returns of the stock and is calculated by dividing today's share price by that of yesterday. *Column (3)* (log *Rt*) is the natural logarithm of share price returns. Notice that column (3) is summed and divided by the number of observations ($n = 25$) so as to give an estimate

Table 7.1: Estimation of volatility, June–November 1995

	(1) S_t	(2) $R_t = S_t/S_{t-1}$	(3) log R_t	(4) log $R_t - u$	(5) log $(R_t - u)^2$
02/Jun./95	83.125				
09/Jun./95	84.875	1.0210526	0.020834	0.018554	0.0003443
16/Jun./95	87.000	1.0250368	0.024729	0.022449	0.0005040
23/Jun./95	91.125	1.0474138	0.046324	0.044044	0.0019399
30/Jun./95	90.375	0.9917695	−0.00826	−0.010544	0.0001112
07/Jul./95	95.625	1.0580913	0.056467	0.054187	0.0029362
14/Jul./95	103.625	1.0836601	0.080344	0.078065	0.0060941
21/Jul./95	92.000	0.8878166	−0.11899	−0.121270	0.0147063
28/Jul./95	92.625	1.0067935	0.006771	0.004491	0.0000202
04/Aug./95	93.875	1.0134953	0.013405	0.011125	0.0001238
11/Aug./95	96.500	1.0279627	0.027579	0.025299	0.0006401
18/Aug./95	97.125	1.0064767	0.006456	0.004176	0.0000174
25/Aug./95	94.375	0.9716860	−0.02872	−0.031002	0.0009611
01/Sep./95	89.750	0.9509934	−0.05025	−0.052528	0.0027592
08/Sep./95	95.500	1.0640669	0.062098	0.059819	0.0035783
15/Sep./95	93.438	0.9784031	−0.02183	−0.024113	0.0005814
22/Sep./95	89.750	0.9605351	−0.04026	−0.042544	0.0018100
29/Sep./95	90.500	1.0083565	0.008322	0.006042	0.0000365
06/Oct./95	85.875	0.9488950	−0.05246	−0.054737	0.0029961
13/Oct./95	86.250	1.0043668	0.004357	0.002078	0.0000043
20/Oct./95	95.500	1.1072464	0.101876	0.099597	0.0099195
27/Oct./95	100.000	1.0471204	0.046044	0.043764	0.0019153
03/Nov./95	99.500	0.9950000	−0.00501	−0.007292	0.0000532
10/Nov./95	96.875	0.9736181	−0.02674	−0.029016	0.0008419
17/Nov./95	87.375	0.9019355	−0.10321	−0.105492	0.0111285
24/Nov./95	88.000	1.0071531	0.007128	0.004848	0.0000235
Sum			0.056991		0.0640463

Mean	= 0.00228
Variance	= 0.002669
Annual variance	= 0.138767
Volatility	= 37.25% p.a.

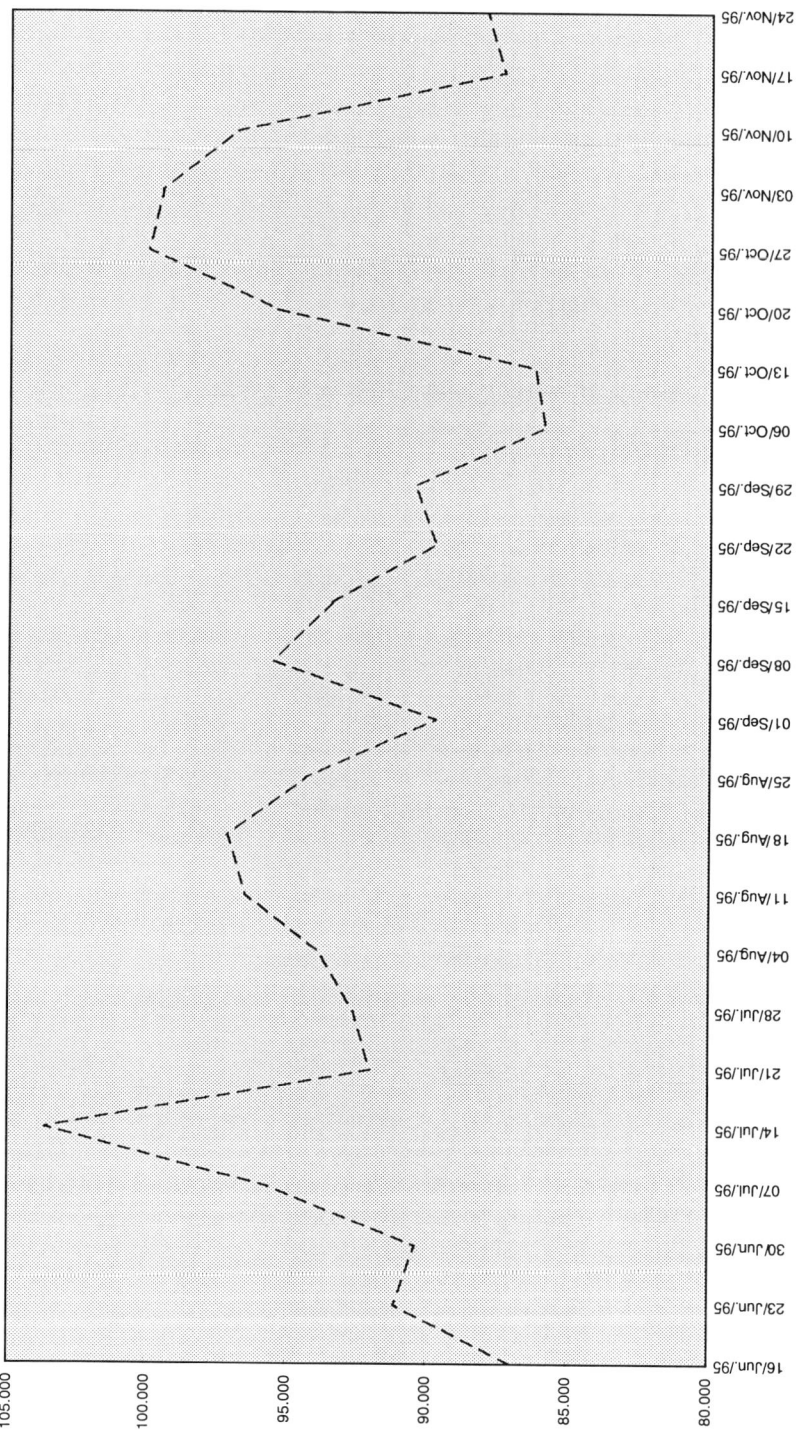

Figure 7.2: Microsoft share price, June–November 1995

98

of the mean (*u*). *Column (4)* (log[*Rt* − *u*]²) is a measure of deviation about the mean, which is summed and then divided by the number of observations adjusted for *n* − 1 degrees of freedom, to give a variance number equal to 0.002669.

In order to annualise the volatility, we multiply by 52. If we were to use monthly or daily data, we would have to use a multiplier of 12 and 250 respectively (there are 250 trading days in a year), thus giving an annual variance of 0.138767. If we take the square root of this number we arrive at the volatility estimate of 37.25% p.a.

It is always useful to simply graph and look at raw data. In order to trade volatility, we need to see substantial movements both up and down. The way we would go about hedging would depend on the path taken by the stock. Figure 7.2 plots the Microsoft share price over the six months under consideration and Figure 7.3 plots the logged returns. If the share was less volatile, then the logged returns would have lower maximum points and larger minimum points. Now plotting the relative frequency distribution in Figure 7.4 is particularly interesting. In the case of the relative frequency distribution, if Microsoft was less volatile then the spread of the distribution would be smaller.

The volatility of Microsoft was 37.25%. Given that the distribution of returns is lognormal, the distribution of logged returns is normal. A feature of the normal distribution is that 67% of the distribution lies within ± one standard deviation. There is a 67% chance that the logged returns of Microsoft will be ±37.25%. If the share price of Microsoft is 90 today, then translated into share price returns, the upper and lower limits are given by:

Upper limit $S \times \exp(+\sigma) = 90 \times 1.45 = 130.5$ (7.3)

Lower limit $S \times \exp(-\sigma) = 90 \times 0.68 = 61.2$ (7.4)

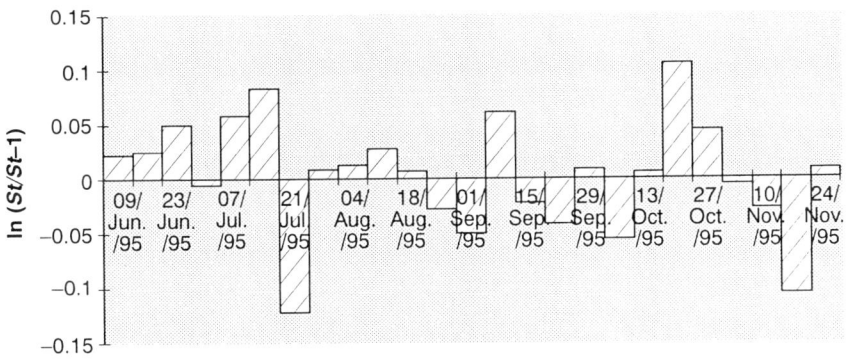

Figure 7.3: Logged returns, June–November 1995

99

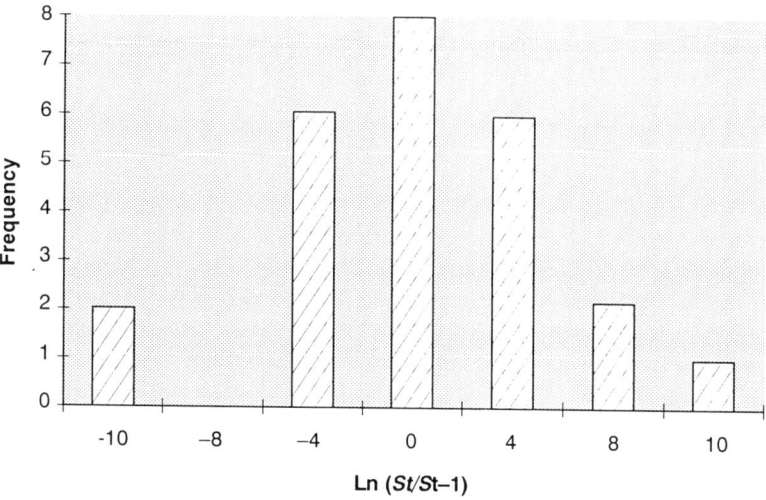

Figure 7.4: Relative frequency distribution

PROBLEMS AND PRACTICAL ISSUES WHEN VALUING CONVERTIBLE BONDS

Dilution

Thus far, we deliberately avoided bringing up a difference between a call option and the call option component of a convertible bond. When a convertible is converted into the underlying equity, it is usually the case that new shares are issued. This is in contrast to the exercise of a call option which involves merely the transaction of second hand shares. Equity is diluted upon conversion of the bond. The pricing of corporate derivatives, such as converts or warrants, still seems to be at the cutting edge of option pricing theory. Many authors, from Galai and Schneller (1978), Cox *et al.* (1985), Subrahmanyam (see Figlewski *et al.*, 1990) to Gemmill (1993) and others, have concentrated on treating the underlying asset of converts and warrants not as the underlying share at all, but rather the *value of the firm*. This is extremely impractical. Over the past twenty-two years, very little headway has been made in the field of corporate derivatives, much of this due to how one should incorporate dilution.

In order to basically understand the issues as presented, think first of a warrant – a call issued by a company exerciseable into newly issued shares at a given price over a given time period. At expiry, it is most commonly shown that:

$$W^* = \{(S^* - X)/(1 + \lambda), 0\} \tag{7.5}$$

Where W^* = warrant price at expiry

S^* = price of one share on expiry, as if no warrants had been issued

X = exercise price

λ = the dilution factor from exercise of warrant

That is, the holder of the warrant will receive the maximum of the diluted difference between the share and exercise price and zero. There are a number of issues here which are rarely brought up or are simply assumed away. First, let's think about when the share price reflects the potential of dilution from the derivative. The share price just does not fall on expiry. The share price is likely to discount the probability of conversion. It is arguable, in fact, that the share price might even possibly reflect the probability of dilution prior to the terms of the deal fixing.

One could calculate the probability of conversion in the following fashion. Referring to Table 4.4 once again (step 10), we know with probability one or zero whether the convertible will be converted. One can now work backwards to arrive at the probability of conversion at each node. This is quite a straightforward procedure but many problems remain unanswered. It would be sensible in our opinion for analysts not to always consider fully diluted earnings per share. For example, if a derivative is 50% out of the money, with just one year to maturity, it is not just conservative to adjust earnings per share by the full extent of dilution, it is incorrect.

The issuance of warrants and convertibles definitely *impacts on the volatility of the underlying share and its likely path*. Most experienced traders of warrants and convertible bonds will have seen the phenomenon of an issue being '*pulled to the money*' as maturity approaches. Consider an example of the Japanese issued *Nankai Electric Railway*, which has 20,000 warrants (as of 20 November 1995), which expire 9 April 1996, each exercisable into 949.1263 shares. On this day, the warrant was 6.3% out of the money. If the share price tried to rise 10%, there would probably be tremendous share selling in as much as the hedge ratio would approach 100%. Gamma is 'peaked' around the money. Dampened volatility is marked in such cases. This is common where companies have issued derivatives which are hedged against stock.

Moreover, one has to consider the reality of companies which have a number of convertibles and warrants outstanding simultaneously. As first noted by Emmanuel (1983a, 1983b), there is an obvious interdependence between different derivatives issued by the same company. In the case of *Nankai Electric Railway*, already noted above for example, there is a further warrant (2 December 1997) which exercises into over 43 million shares and a convertible bond (2.7% 30 March 2001) which converts into over 45 million shares. Total outstanding potential dilution then equates to more than 23% given that there were 460 million shares outstanding already.

Theoretical Spread

For those who worked through the theoretical pricing of converts, an obvious stumbling block came to light. This related to the degree by which the straight bond equivalent security trades above the riskless rate assumed. This is referred to as the credit adjusted spread or theoretical spread and was the subject matter of Chapter 6. In fact, this turned out not to be a tremendous problem in practice.

It is fair to say at this stage that at very low share prices relative to the conversion price, the spread tends to widen in practice. This will reflect the market's perception of the company's ability to meet future coupon payments as well as the redemption proceeds. Of course, it further brings to light that it may be necessary to discount coupon payments at the risky rate even if there is a 100% hedge versus the underlying equity. This, of course, can easily be catered for given the approach we have taken to price the instruments thus far. Moreover, it was shown in Chapter 6 that the theoretical spread is also a non-linear function of time. That is to say, the risky rate assigned will differ if there is only six months to maturity rather than, say, ten years, as well as being dependent on other factors.

Multi-Factor Analysis

One can incorporate a multi-factor analysis of convertible securities rather than the single factor model used. That is, one need not only consider share prices following a particular process over a given time period. Interest rates need not necessarily be held constant over time. c.f. Ho and Lee (1986). In practice, nevertheless, this complicates analysis considerably and does not tend to benefit pricing very much.

Volatility Known and Constant

An assumption made in the analysis presented in Chapter 4 was that of known and constant volatility. But anyone familiar with estimating or monitoring volatility of particular shares will know that the measure does in fact change over time. However, the estimates do appear to change slowly. Markets go through extremely volatile and then extremely quiet periods. Changes in volatility appears to be largely random rather than systematic. That is volatility appears to be *stochastic*.

Over the years, many models have been adapted which cater for differing features of volatility but the model presented so far not only benefits from parsimony, it actually will model well in practice. Because of their longer lives, convertibles and warrants generally are not terribly sensitive to 'blips' in short term volatility estimates. The consensus appears to have emerged that the impact of changes in volatility being random is not absolutely vital.

A number of key features have considerable practical applicability nonetheless. The first relates to what is known as *mean reversion*. Throughout any crash type situation in equity markets such as 'Black Monday' in 1987, or the Tokyo stock market crash in 1990, many individual volatilities were fantastically high, even exceeding 100%, but it was just a question of time before they reverted to a mean level. The same applies to commodities, such as the price of oil during the Gulf War.

Figure 7.5 is replicated from Gemmill's *Options Pricing*, and is very interesting with reference to converts.

The fact is that, from experience in convertible and warrant markets, the point to focus on is that implieds on the longer dated maturities reflect the fact that the market anticipates mean reversion. Figure 7.5 could actually be extended out to longer dates.

The second point of note relates to the fact that the volatilities of individual shares have a tendency to move in the same direction. This makes sense. Just as with share movement, some of which is explained by company or industry specific information and some of which is explained by the market in general, the same applies to volatility.

The third point to note is that changes in share prices tend to be *inversely* related to changes in volatilities. This is found not only for individual shares but also for market indexes as well. The reason most often given for this is that when share prices fall/rise, the debt/equity ratio rises/falls, thus making the equity more/less risky. This points to return distributions being *skewed*.

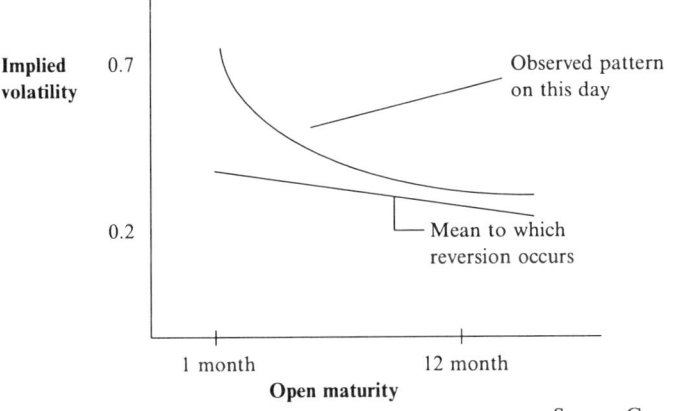

Source: Gemmill (1993).

Figure 7.5: The concept of mean reversion

Moreover, there tends to be a bias toward share prices rising in the long run.

We saw that volatility was used in the binomial model in the determination of the up ('*u*') and down ('*d*') factors of the underlying equity tree in Chapter 4. Often overlooked from an academic standpoint, but of crucial importance in practice, is the fact that rehedging does not actually take place at each node, as is theoretically assumed. Transactions costs are not zero – the question of when to rehedge will shortly be addressed.

Lognormal Distribution of Stock Returns

The assumption of lognormality is an extension of the binomial process. The assumption is used widely when pricing options. Both practitioners and writers find that tails of the actual distribution are slightly fatter than that of the lognormal and this bias tends to cause mispricing of deep in and deep out of the money examples – they tend to look a little expensive. This feature of the distribution is referred to as *leptokurtosis* (see Figure 7.6). This is probably due to the fact that there is actually a jump diffusion process, or that there are a number of normal distributions which have different variance. This particular problem may be more exaggerated with corporate derivatives because of issues raised above under equity dilution.

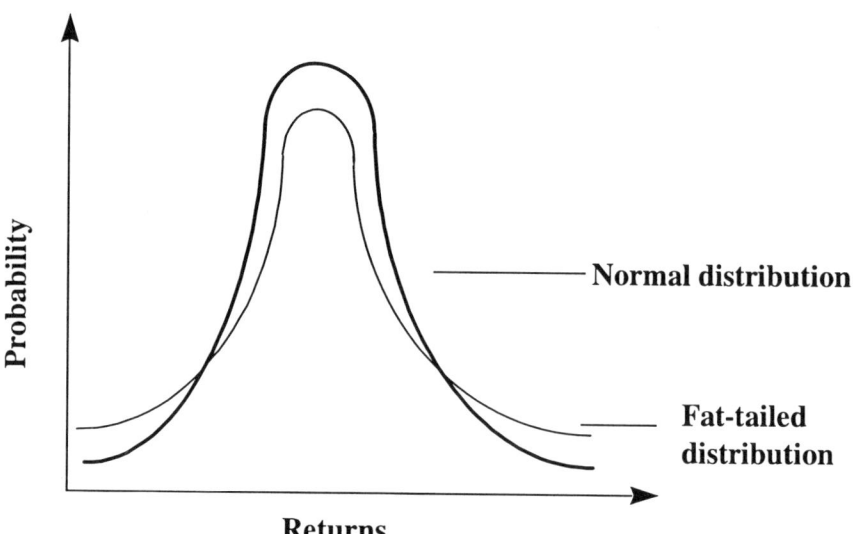

Figure 7.6: Actual distribution versus normal distribution

IMPLIED VOLATILITY

It is relatively straightforward to arrive at all inputs into the binomial model of Chapter 4. The theoretical spread may be a little awkward at times, but this was addressed in Chapter 6. As we can see from this chapter, volatility is of crucial concern to us. What if we assume therefore that the actual price of any given convertible is fair and solve for volatility in the model?

In other words, let's see what annualised volatility of the underlying share is being *implied* by the convert.

We know from Chapter 4 that:

$$CB = f(S, R, T, C, \sigma, d, c, p) \tag{7.6}$$

where CB = Convertible bond price
   S = Share price
   R = Interest rates
   T = Time to maturity
   C = Coupon
   σ = Volatility of the underlying share
   d = Dividend yield
   c = call provision
   p = put provision

We now wish to consider:

$$\textbf{Implied volatility} = g\,(S,\,R,\,T,\,C,\,d,\,c,\,p,\,CB) \tag{7.7}$$

The exact functional form of this is unknown, but we can solve for the implied by using an iterative procedure, such as Newton–Raphson (usually arrives at the implied by three searches).

Let's reconsider the callable–puttable bond that we priced theoretically in Chapter 4, which had a fair value of 117.44, as can be seen from Table 7.2. In arriving at this fair value, various assumptions have been made, one of the most important of which is that the volatility of the underlying share is 20% per annum.

Let's say that the actual market price of this instrument was 126. In other words, the bond appears to be more than eight points overvalued. What volatility would the share have to exhibit for this instrument not to be overpriced? It certainly would have to be greater than 20%. In other words, what volatility is the instrument implying? Look at Table 7.3.

In this example then, the fair value equals the actual market price when we assume the volatility of the underlying share is 35.75%.

Table 7.2: Example of puttable/callable CB pricing

NS	0	1	2	3	4	5	6	7	8	9	10
0	117.44	127.11	140.50	159.91	185.83	217.72	253.33	296.52	345.33	403.95	470.76
1		112.62	117.62	125.80	139.78	163.95	190.54	223.22	259.75	304.02	354.09
2			110.61	112.77	115.75	127.50	143.32	168.08	195.37	228.86	266.33
3				111.32	112.77	114.24	115.75	126.61	146.95	172.33	200.33
4					112.77	114.24	115.75	104.52	110.53	129.80	150.68
5						114.24	115.75	98.62	101.29	105.60	113.33
6							115.75	97.18	98.35	99.54	100.75
7								97.18	98.35	99.54	100.75
8									98.35	99.54	100.75
9										99.54	100.75
10											100.75

Table 7.3: Volatility and fair value

Iterations	Volatility	Fair value
1	30	122.99
2	40	128.66
3	35.75	126.00

TRADING VOLATILITY AND ESTABLISHMENT OF A MARKET NEUTRAL HEDGE

It is necessary but not sufficient to be able to value the convertible bond when hedging. It is of absolute importance to be able to first ascertain how to extract the arbitrage profit, and secondly we should be in a position to be able to decompose profit and loss from the strategy.

In simple terms, a good deal of participants view the process of hedging as follows: 'Buy an "undervalued" security versus the short sale of a security which is more expensive and wait until repricing occurs'. In practice, there have been sustained periods where the undervalued security has become even cheaper. Markets have suffered premium compression. Our view of the nature of this trade may be very different. The objective of the arbitrage is to capture the difference between the actual and fair values through the implementation of systematic trading. It is possible to exploit the incorrect curvature of the option via trading of volatility and in the process we do not have to rely on repricing itself.

The success of the strategy should not depend on the convertible bond approaching its fair value in the market place – the security may trade at a theoretical discount. Far too much attention normally focuses on issues such as whether thirty day or fifty day estimates of volatility are best, or whether we should be using exponentially smoothed, robust estimates of volatility – this is understandable in the context of trading exchange options, not convertibles. It comes down to really understanding the core basis of how arbitrage profits are derived. It is with this in mind that fund management and proprietary trading characteristics of *strict discipline* and *consistency* need to be emphasised.

The hedge strategy thrives on uncertainty in markets, as reflected by volatility of the financial instruments concerned. The strategy is therefore said to be 'long volatility'. Convertible bonds are typically long dated and as such interest rates and associated cost of carry are key determinants of pricing and expected profit/loss (see Figure 7.7).

Figure 7.7 clearly illustrates how an arbitrage profit should be derived from an undervalued warrant or convertible bond via the trading of volatility. It is assumed that the security in question has a delta or hedge ratio of 50%. That is, for infinitesimally small changes in the share price, the convertible price captures 50% of the underlying share's movement. In order to take a delta neutral stance, two bonds are held long for every one share sold short. If we now consider a large move in the share of ±100 units, it can be seen that the convertible gains/losses are more/less than the share. In this first hypothetical case, a profit of 20 units is made irrespective of whether the share advances or declines.

If the share price advances 100 units and then subsequently retreats by the same amount, no gains are made unless adjustments are made to the position. It should be obvious that we become long in advancing markets and short in declining markets. In order to achieve the goal of realising arbitrage gains, we

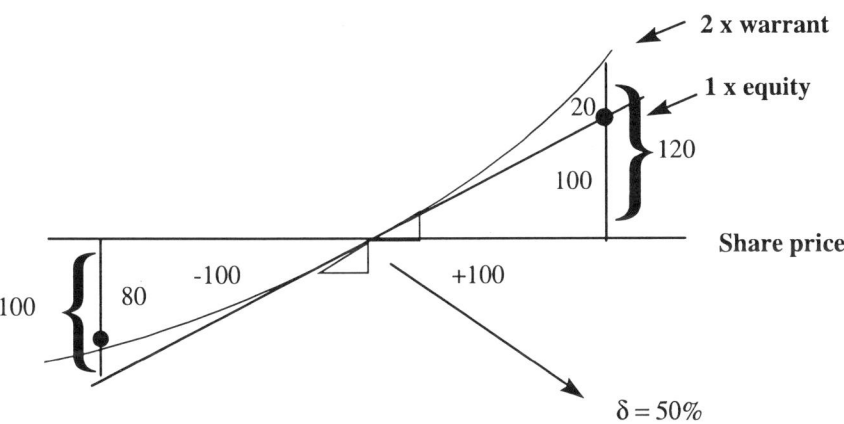

Figure 7.7: Concept of long volatility

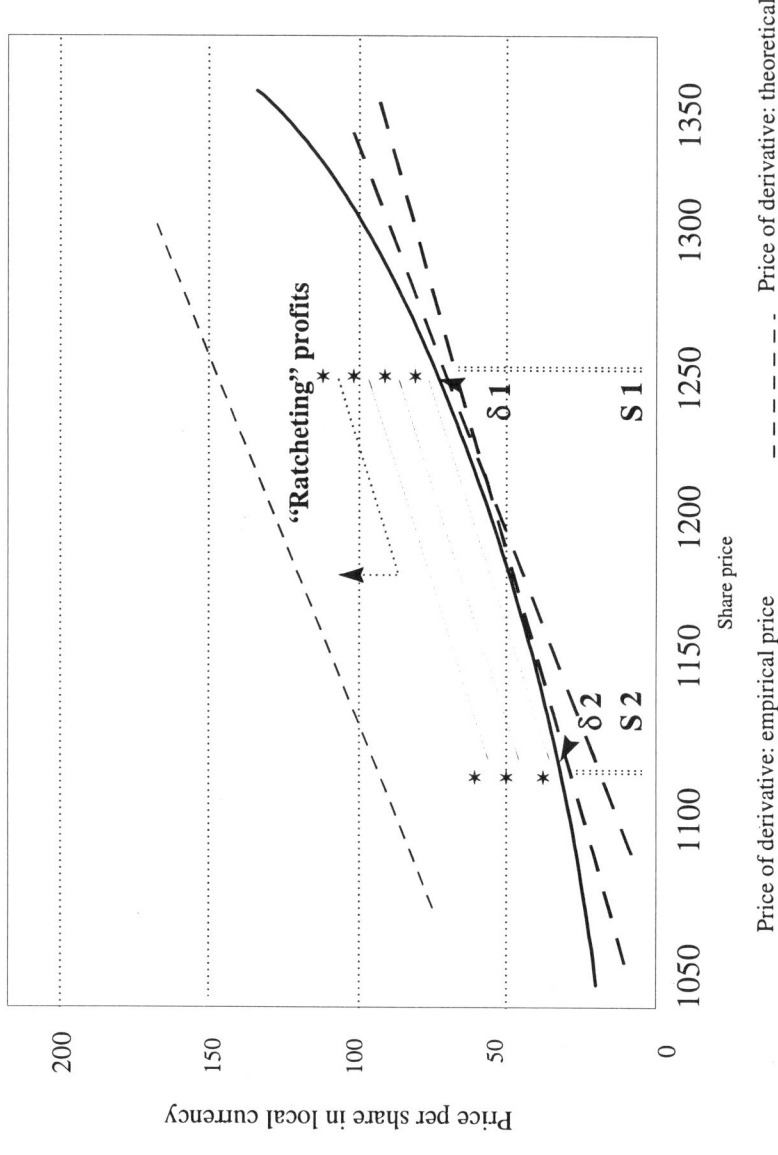

Figure 7.8: Magnified section of price curve – dynamic rehedging

need to sell convertible bonds/shares given equity advances and buy convertible bonds/shares for equity declines. The amount by which we adjust is dictated by the delta function of the security.

Irrespective of how simple this process appears, it is the heart of option pricing and needs to be emphasised accordingly. We should therefore view the process of convertible arbitrage as providing for an *'income flow'* over time. If we were to take a long position versus a delta adjusted short and dynamically adjust the position, the return profile should *replicate the return to fixed income* if the derivative is fairly priced. That is, we can synthesise fixed income using fairly priced derivatives and the underlying share.

It would be useful for us to consider Figure 7.8. This graph is conceptual but is particularly helpful in showing how readjusting provides for a 'ratcheting' towards the fair price from a volatility aspect alone. The interesting point is that the derivative security need not necessarily become more expensive. Delta neutral positions of $\delta 1$ and $\delta 2$ are assumed at share prices $S1$ and $S2$ respectively. Given that the share prices move back and forth continually, gains from trading are summed above the actual price in order to give an impression of how income flows from volatility enable the ratcheting process to take place.

PREMIUM COMPRESSION

In practice, of course, despite trading cheap, a convertible bond may still suffer premium compression. Figure 7.9 illustrates that a consistent and systematic approach under such circumstances should result in an *increased expected return* from the investment strategy: this results from the increased 'gamma' of the investment. Gamma may be defined as the rate of change of delta with respect to an infinitesimally small change in the underlying share price. The strategies outlined are 'long volatility', and *'long gamma'*.

The initial hedged position is assumed to be established at point A. The share price increases to B where no profit is experienced due to premium compression. It is shown how the expected profit increases as a result of increased convexity if the share declines to point A. It is difficult for hedge fund managers or proprietary traders when faced with this whole issue. It is often said that one should simply increase the hedge investment – this is really avoiding the question of what to do with the existing position. Once again, this is really all about decomposing profit and loss, as well as applying consistency.

Example
Let's consider an example, not for simulation purposes, but because it raises a number of theoretical and practical issues. We are going to focus on *Fujitsu*

109

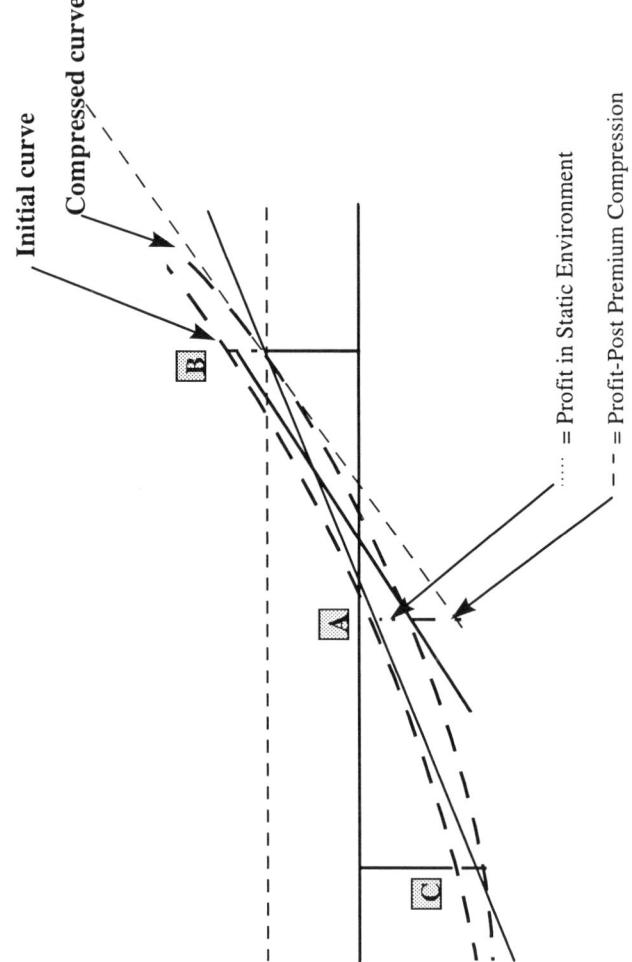

Figure 7.9: 'Premium compression' with increasing gamma

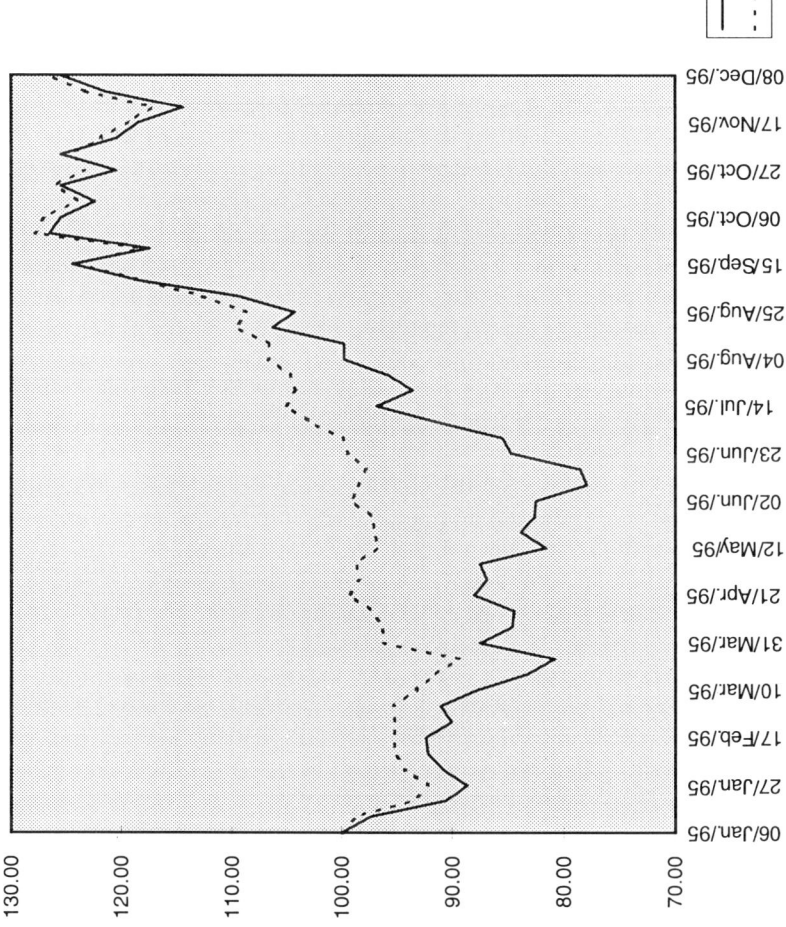

Figure 7.10: Equity and convertible bond returns to Fujitsu Ltd, 6 January 1995–8 December 1995

over the period 6 January 1995 to the end of December 1995. Figure 7.10 plots the returns to an outright equity or convert holder over the whole period. For the equity holder, there is a 22.1% decline in the investment value over the period 6 January to 9 June, followed by a retracement of 61% up to December 1995. The convertible bond declines 10.6% to a low of 90.1 on 24 March and then increases 41.5% to 127.5 on 8 December. These are typical return profiles to equity and convertible bond investors respectively. The returns profile to a hedge investor should be different. The returns should not go up *or* down because of directional movements in the market but rather because the market goes up *and* down.

Let's assume that on 6 January 1995, Investor *A* believes Fujitsu no. 8 1.9% 29 March 2002 to be interesting from a hedge perspective. The relevant terms for this issue are as in Table 7.4.

The raw data used in this example is given in Table 7.5.

On 6 January 1995, the convertible bond price closed at 100.8 (i.e. Yen 1,008,000) on the Tokyo Stock Exchange. On the same day, the share price closed at Yen 988. The fair price for the bond is calculated at 116. The historic volatility was estimated at 25%. The benchmark yield on the *Japan Government Bond* (5.5% 09/20/2002) was 4.53% on this day and 3 month yen 'London Interbank Offer Rate' (LIBOR) was 2.44%. Mikuni rate the bond 'AA'. We assume a gross theoretical spread of 50 basis points over Japanese governments of similar maturity. The bond floor was estimated to be around 87.5% and parity was equal to 99%. Diagrammatically, the issue would look as depicted in Figure 7.11, versus its theoretical valuation.

There is always an element of subjectivity in the deltas or hedge ratios to actually use. After all, if the bond is cheap and future adjustments are made with the instrument trading cheaply, there is an element of error in the sensitivity ratio. For this reason, market practitioners often introduce an element of empiricism.

Table 7.4: Fujitsu issue, terms

Quick code	:	(6702)
Borrower	:	Fujitsu Ltd
Coupon	:	1.9%
Maturity	:	29 March 2002 at 'par'
Denomination	:	Yen 1,000,000
Shares per bond	:	1,002.004
First coupon	:	31 March 1995
Rating	:	AA Mikuni

Table 7.5: Raw data for Fujitsu example

	Equity	% change	Delta	Convert	2002 JGB	Yield	LIBOR
06/Jan./95	988	0.0	0.75	100.80	105.519	4.530	2.438
13/Jan./95	962	−2.6	0.75	99.50	106.145	4.425	2.375
20/Jan./95	895	−9.4	0.75	94.30	105.773	4.485	2.313
27/Jan./95	876	−11.3	0.68	93.00	106.088	4.430	2.313
03/Feb./95	898	−9.1	0.68	95.00	105.839	4.470	2.313
10/Feb./95	911	−7.8	0.68	96.00	106.059	4.430	2.313
17/Feb./95	913	−7.6	0.68	96.00	106.500	4.355	2.313
24Feb./95	890	−9.9	0.68	96.00	107.172	4.240	2.313
03/Mar./95	900	−8.9	0.68	96.00	108.002	4.105	2.313
10/Mar./95	867	−12.2	0.68	94.00	108.734	3.985	2.188
17/Mar./95	822	−16.8	0.68	92.20	110.087	3.770	2.188
24/Mar./95	798	−19.2	0.60	90.10	110.847	3.650	2.125
31/Mar./95	865	−12.4	0.60	97.00	112.253	3.430	1.766
07/Apr./95	836	−15.4	0.60	97.10	113.246	3.280	1.688
14Apr./95	834	−15.6	0.60	98.10	114.304	3.120	1.625
21/Apr./95	870	−11.9	0.60	100.20	113.572	3.220	1.438
28/Apr./95	859	−13.1	0.60	99.20	113.619	3.210	1.438
05/May/95	865	−12.4	0.60	99.50	113.422	3.235	1.313
12/May/95	806	−18.4	0.60	97.50	114.085	3.135	1.375
19/May/95	828	−16.2	0.60	97.80	115.155	2.975	1.375
26/May/95	816	−17.4	0.60	98.00	116.739	2.740	1.313
02/Jun./95	815	−17.5	0.60	99.90	116.618	2.755	1.188
09/Jun./95	770	−22.1	0.49	99.30	117.051	2.690	1.188
16/Jun./95	776	−21.5	0.49	98.60	116.364	2.780	1.188
23/Jun./95	837	−15.3	0.49	100.20	118.654	2.455	1.188
30/Jun./95	845	−14.5	0.49	100.70	118.149	2.515	1.250
07/Jul./95	903	−8.6	0.59	103.70	119.843	2.280	0.875
14/Jul./95	957	−3.1	0.59	105.90	116.862	2.690	0.938
21/Jul./95	925	−6.4	0.59	105.00	117.037	2.655	0.875
28/Jul./95	946	−4.3	0.59	105.50	117.477	2.590	0.812
04/Aug./95	986	−0.2	0.59	107.40	115.885	2.815	0.813
11/Aug./95	986	−0.2	0.65	107.40	115.222	2.905	0.875
18/Aug./95	1050	6.3	0.65	110.50	113.761	3.120	0.938
25/Aug./95	1030	4.3	0.65	109.50	114.433	3.050	0.875
01/Sep./95	1080	9.3	0.70	113.60	115.128	2.900	0.797
08/Sep./95	1170	18.4	0.70	119.10	116.048	2.760	0.563
15/Sep./95	1230	24.5	0.77	125.00	117.504	2.545	0.547
22/Sep./95	1160	17.4	0.77	119.20	118.520	2.395	0.484
29/Sep./95	1250	26.5	0.77	128.80	118.416	2.400	0.469
06/Oct./95	1240	25.5	0.77	128.00	118.286	2.415	0.445
13/Oct./95	1210	22.5	0.77	125.00	118.220	2.420	0.406
20/Oct./95	1240	25.5	0.77	126.90	117.937	2.450	0.367
27/Oct./95	1190	20.4	0.77	124.40	118.017	2.435	0.500
03/Nov./95	1240	25.5	0.77	125.50	118.298	2.385	0.508
10/Nov./95	1190	20.4	0.77	122.80	118.465	2.355	0.453
17/Nov./95	1170	18.4	0.77	120.30	118.377	2.365	0.453
24Nov./95	1130	14.4	0.77	118.00	119.217	2.240	0.484
01/Dec./95	1200	21.5	0.77	124.30	119.115	2.245	0.469
08/Dec./95	1240	25.5	0.77	127.50	119.326	2.210	0.461

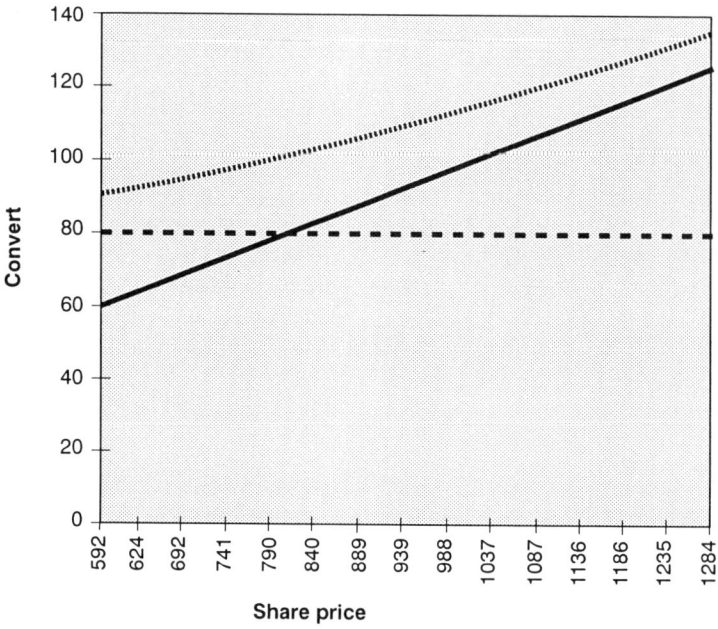

Figure 7.11: Fujitsu no. 8, convertible bond pricing, 6 January 1995

The theoretical delta function is given in Figure 7.12. Now, if the share price of Fujitsu was to increase 10% and we assume the issue will trade at parity, from a conservative standpoint, then the hedge would 'break-even' on an 81% hedge ratio. Using break-even hedge ratios for discrete movements in the stock price is particularly useful. We actually use a hedge ratio of 75% in our example.

In order to establish a 'market neutral' position, versus a long position of 500 bonds (long proceeds equal Yen 504 million), our investor would need to borrow 376,000 shares, thus enabling them to effectively deliver the shares against an effective short sale of the same number of shares in the market at Yen 988. The short proceeds therefore equate to approximately Yen 371 million. The process and cost of borrowing shares will be addressed shortly.

The investor is now market neutral for small moves in the underlying share. It is useful to think of the picture of the magnified section of the price curve in Figure 7.8, so as to appreciate when to adjust. In practice, it usually makes sense to adjust for underlying share moves between 8–12% in price. Of course, in actuality, this will depend very much on the gamma characteristics of the instrument under consideration. and to what extent the bond reprices or becomes cheaper in the process.

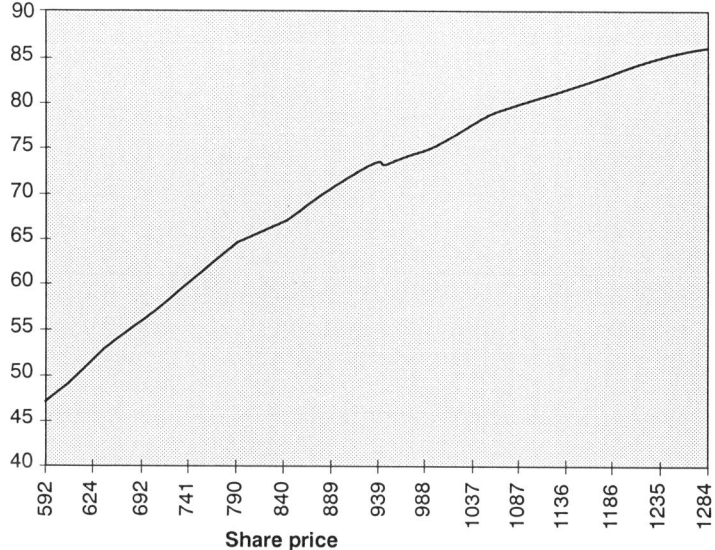

Figure 7.12: Fujitsu no. 8, theoretical delta function at beginning of period

Market etiquette and dealing practices are important since transactions costs can quickly eat into performance. At the same time, there is a cost to dealing in the market place and we should not miss out on very profitable arbitrage opportunities as a result of being overly cautious.

The final piece of the puzzle that needs to be assessed relates to interest rate risk. Over the period under consideration, the underlying *2002 5.5% Japanese Government Bond* (JGB) traded up from 103.376 to 113.810, as can be seen from Figure 7.13. In addition, long and short end yields are plotted in Figure 7.14. Short term rates are important, as will be seen when we look at leverage. As it happens, the shift in the yield curves is relatively parallel.

There are many hedge funds who decide not to hedge interest rate risks, whether at the short or long end. Investors in such funds should be aware that although such investments may be stock market neutral they are not hedged against shifts in the bond market. We therefore need to be aware of the interest rate sensitivity of the bond and be able to monitor it in a dynamic environment of equity and interest rate shifts. When we take a look at the move in the bond market in this case, as shown in Figure 7.14, it seems a pity that we hedged the move, but we follow procedures methodically. The interest rate sensitivity of the convert was estimated as shown in Chapter 5. There was no seven year JGB future, so in this case the ten year contract was used.

From 6 January to 27 January, the share price of Fujitsu falls from Yen 988 to Yen 876 and as the share price falls, the convertible declines at a decreasing

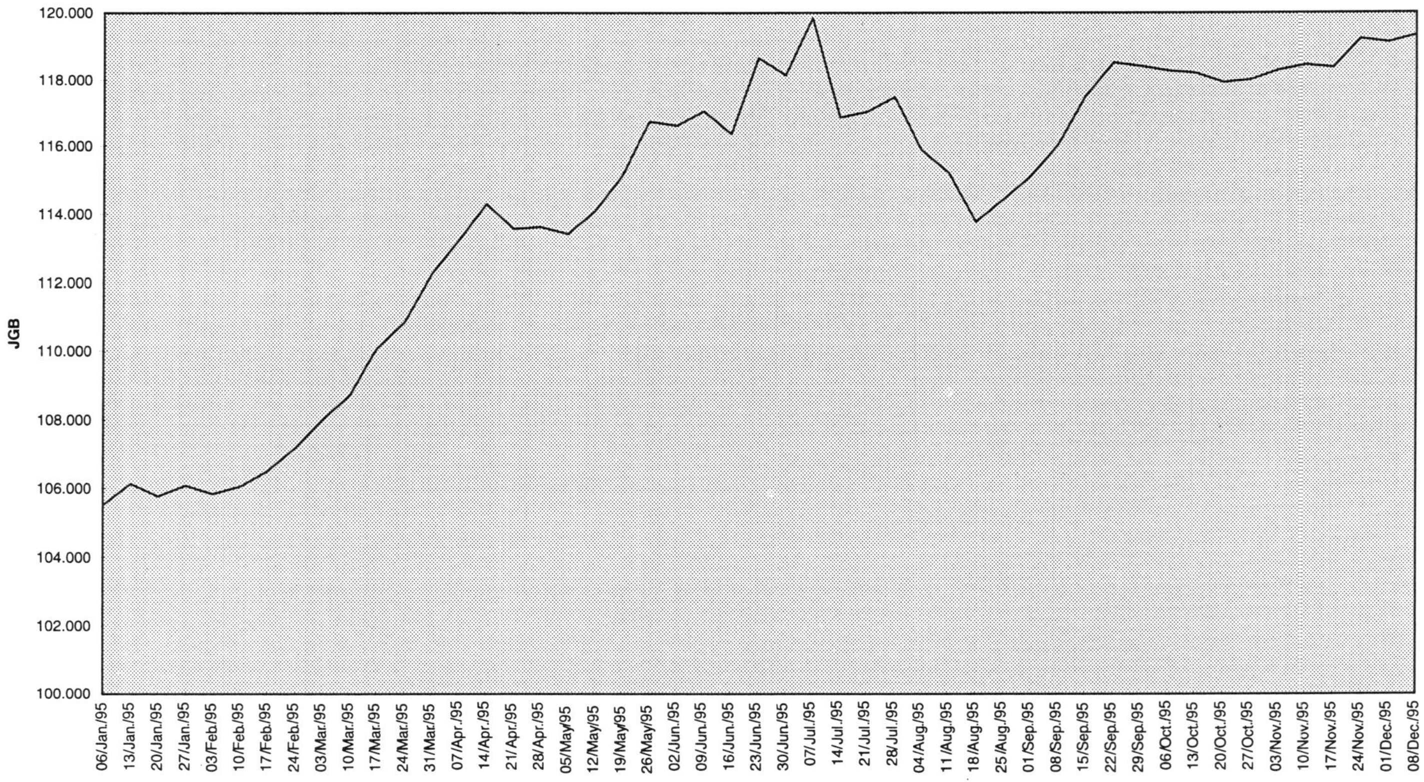

116

Figure 7.13: 2002 5.5% JGB, January–December 1995

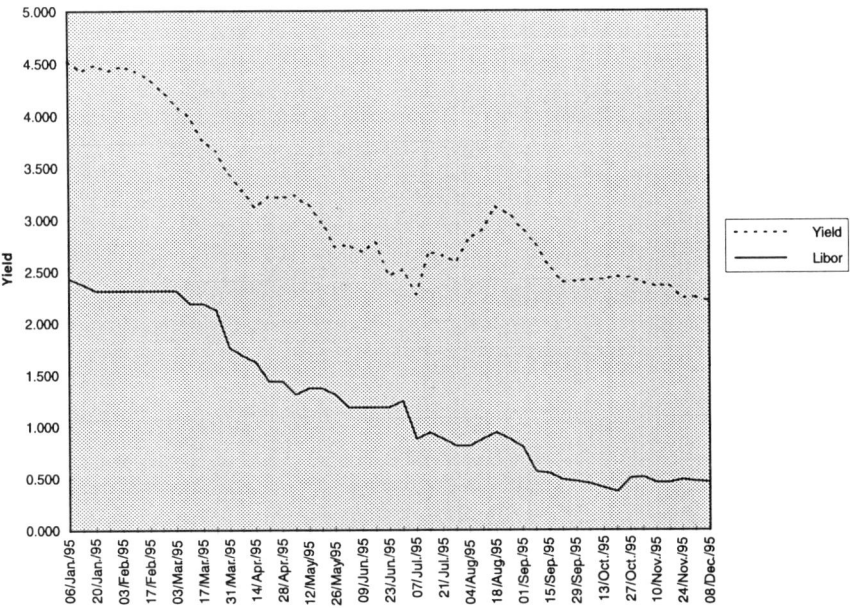

Figure 7.14: Shifts in the short and long Yen yield curves, January–December 1995

pace. This is as one might expect given the delta function already outlined. In terms of exposure, this is equivalent to holding a position in a share and selling some shares on share price declines. One becomes short on share price declines and long on share price advances. In order to rebalance the hedge and effectively 'ratchet' one step toward the correct volatility, we have to buy shares. The new delta is calculated at 68%. One therefore has to buy 35,000 shares at a price of Yen 876. The important point is that we are not buying shares because we believe that the price will 'bounce'. We are merely bringing ourselves back to a market neutral stance.

The Fujitsu bond was cheap from a volatility stand point. As well as volatility, we need to consider income flows which result from 'carry' considerations. Referring right the way back to Chapter 1, we know that deep in the money, the convert should reflect coupon payments *less* dividends. The coupon on Fujitsu no. 8 was 1.9% paid semi-annually and the dividend on the stock was Yen 10 paid twice yearly. It will be shown below, using an example of leverage, that the Fujitsu bond would not have been considered attractive in terms of carry conditions.

As can be seen from Table 7.5, the hedge is adjusted twice over the period 6 January 1995 to 9 June. Over this period, the Fujitsu no. 8 convertible became considerably more expensive and was trading close to its fair value at this

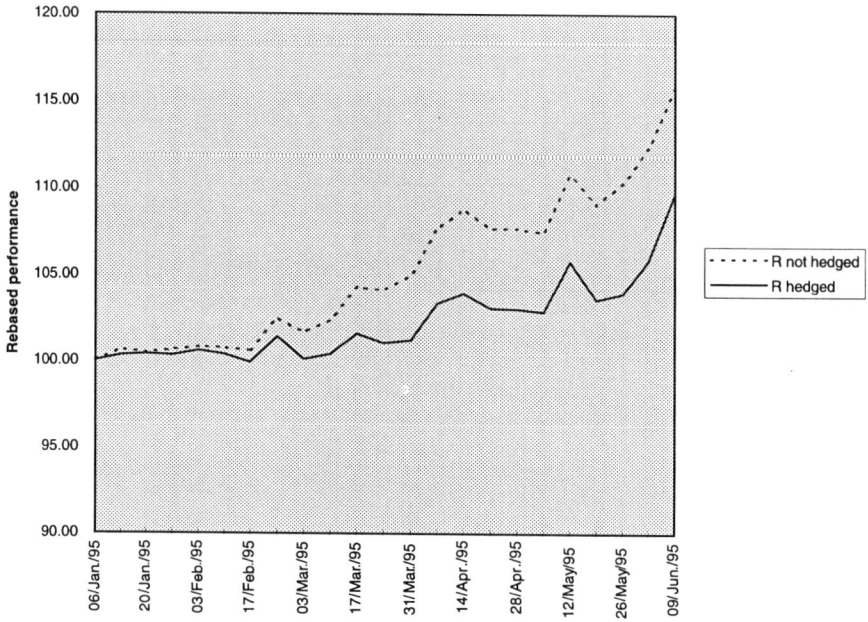

Figure 7.15: Hedge profit profile, January–June 1995

point. For this reason, it would have made sense to unwind the position and lock in to arbitrage gains. Hedgers are often faced with the question of whether they should unwind a position or whether they should continue to trade long volatility. Sometimes profits may be due to carry considerations or simply the gamma characteristics of the bond. On the other hand, if the bond simply goes a long way in terms of repricing, it may make sense to simply use capital more effectively. Fujitsu was an example of the latter. As already mentioned, the answers to such questions are often a function of the amount of capital and its cost to different hedge fund managers.

Figure 7.15 illustrates the unleveraged profit and loss profile to the hedger, by trading volatility with and without interest rate risk hedged, over the months January to June.

We are now in a position to consider the leveraged outlook to this investment strategy, as well as some of the practical decisions taken in practice by hedgers. Consider Table 7.6 which illustrates a typical cost of carry and leverage on the bond for a hedge fund as of 6 January 1995.

Basic terms are first listed. On the long side, we hold 500 bonds of Yen 1000,000 nominal value each, with a total market value of Yen 504,000,000. On the short side, given an initial hedge ratio of 75% or 376,000 shares totalling Yen 371,000,000. Margins on hedged positions differ according to the

Table 7.6: Cost of carry and leverage on CBs

Issuer		Fujitsu Ltd no. 8	1.9%	29//Mar./02		
Strike	:	998	Share price	:		998
Ratio	:	1,002.004	Bond price	:		100.80%
Denomin.	:	1,000,000	Parity	:		99.00%
S/E	:	0.99	Premium	:		1.82%
Long position	:		Short position	:		
Nominal	:	1,000,000	Delta	:		75.00%
Market value	:	504,000,000	Shares short	:		375,752
No. of bonds	:	500	Proceeds Yen	:		371,242,485
MARGIN REQUIREMENT						
PREMIUM	:	13,652	UNHEDGED %	:		25.00%
		13,652	UNHEDGED TOTAL	:		126,000,000
10% OF HEDGE	:	37,800,00	30% MARGIN	:		37,800,000
		13,652				
TOTAL MARGIN	:	37,813,652	BOND POINTS	:		7.50%
GEARING	:	13.3				
LIBID ON SHORT	:	2.250%	LIBOR	:		2.313%
LOAN RATE	:	1.000%	CLIENT OVER	:		1.250%
MARGIN DEBIT	:	466,186,348	DDEBIT RATE	:		3.563%
COST MAR DEB	:	(46,139)				
SHORT REBATE	:	12,890				
YIELD	:	26,389				
Dividend	:	(10,438)				
CASH FLOW	:	(17,298)				
ANNUAL FLOW	:	(2,469,689)				

particular or financing house concerned, the credit rating/amount of business conducted by the investor. Those who have access to better financing are likely to be at a great advantage. In our example, we assume it is calculated in a manner common to most.

25% (i.e. 1 − delta) of the market value of the bonds is unhedged in the case of Fujitsu. Let's say 30% of this is considered as margin required. The lesser of premium or 10% of the hedge is added to this amount to give a total margin required. It should be apparent that if premium is low and the delta high, leverage will be very large. In fact, when delta is 100% and premium is zero, the margin is zero. It is useful for brokers to understand when recommending issues that the effective carry for new hedge funds with limited funds under management is a crucial concern.

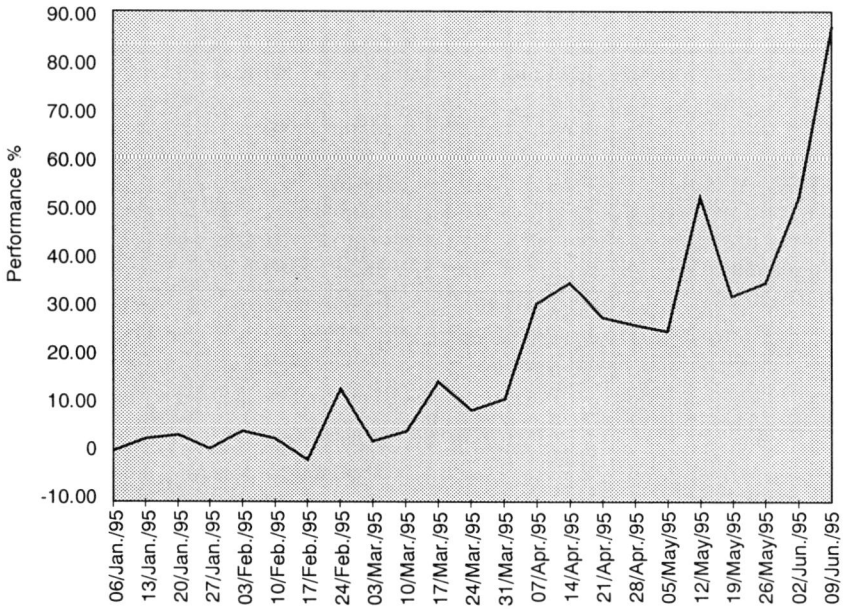

Figure 7.16: Returns to hedge on leverage and unleveraged basis, January–June 1995

Our investor receives the 'London Interbank Bid Rate' (LIBID) on the short proceeds, *less* the loan rate multiplied by short proceeds. On the other hand, our investor pays LIBOR, plus an addition dependent on his own rating (e.g. 125 basis points) on the margin debit (market value *less* total margin). The daily and annual flows are then outlined.

Some convertibles are purely 'carry plays'. They finance 'positively' on a leveraged basis. Others may be dependent on volatility to make a profitable return to arbitrage. As regards our Fujitsu example, the leveraged profit and loss profile, assuming that we hedge interest rate risk, is shown in Figure 7.16. This, of course, is an isolated example, but we would find that as we diversified our hedge portfolio by increasing more and more issues, the profile would become less volatile. Moreover, it is important to bear the following point in mind. There are benefits which come from being hedged across the share price/ investment value range. For example, a well diversified portfolio might contain issues which are on the one hand deeper in the money and carry well but are essentially 'synthetic puts' in nature. On the other hand, it might also contain positions which are trading relatively close to their floors and in this sense are much more 'call orientated'.

There are many other practical considerations which need to be borne in mind when hedging versus stock. It is surprisingly important to be aware of new issues as soon as possible. Those funds who are on top of new issues will also be first to locate 'pools' of equity to be borrowed, and therefore be in a position to hedge those converts which offer better value. As soon as most issues are announced, hedge funds scurry to identify shares to be utilised given anticipated allocations.

Another important practical consideration relates to whether stock is '*callable*'. As the term suggests, callable stock is understood to be much more short term orientated and indicates that it is far more likely to be taken away from the borrower. This would leave the hedger with a naked long position and subject to market risk.

CONCLUDING REMARKS

This chapter has set out to study the nature of volatility and how we might benefit from trading it. It has given us an opportunity to pull together a great deal of work developed in earlier chapters, ranging from issues as basic as minimum arbitrage boundaries, to fair pricing, sensitivity ratios, and interest rate hedging. Many hedge type strategies are sold as 'black box' trading, with very little explanation of the underlying mechanisms involved, as we would expect. However, at the same time it is important that investors and traders of such funds are aware of what risks should be noted.

8: Multivariate Hedging

INTRODUCTION

In Chapter 7, we considered the establishment of a market neutral hedge strategy using a long convertible bond position versus the short sale of the same underlying equity. This is the most common type of hedge or long volatility position and may be thought of as *univariate*. In contrast, this chapter introduces *multivariate* hedging, an area of study which has received very little written attention, but has been utilised particularly by 'larger' investors eager to overcome certain difficulties or disadvantages of conventional hedging. Understandably, this type of hedging has been eschewed by many investors, particularly by smaller funds or by larger funds not prepared to take on the more uncertain return profile.

Multivariate hedging involves taking a long position in more than one security versus the short sale of an individual composite security. So, for example, it might take the form of a purchase of warrants, options, convertibles and equity versus the short sale of a given index future. Many preconceived views of the trade exist, ranging from the issue of 'beta' adjustments, minimum tracking tolerance levels, and the delta adjustment procedure. Of course, in addition to using the framework to hedge, it may similarly be used to synthesise an outright equity position. For this reason, the analysis will be relevant to equity fund managers who wish to gain exposure to given market places.

Before addressing many of the interesting aspects that arise from this 'basket' type hedging, we first simply review why a portfolio of options will always be more valuable than a composite index option on the same set of equities. This is done because it has related properties to many issues raised. We then go on to consider an unrealistic, but simplified example of a basket trade, before addressing issues of tracking error, portfolio selection, adjustments, as well as actual returns experienced to this kind of trading.

A PORTFOLIO OF INDIVIDUAL OPTIONS VERSUS AN INDEX OPTION

Let's think of an example. The Nikkei 225 stock index is price weighted. If it were the case that each share which goes to make up the index had an outstanding at the money listed option, then when added together the value of these should never be less than an individual index option on the Nikkei 225. This should seem obvious. After all, an index option will either expire in *or* out of the money. On the other hand, if we were to compare this with a portfolio of individual options on shares which go to make up the same index, some might expire out of the money while others will expire in the money. It is unlikely that each and every option will expire out of or in the money. The extent to which more or less options actually expire in or out of the money will depend on the *correlation* between the shares concerned.

If an Index (I) is composed of N shares, and its value is equal to the sum of N shares (S), with respective weightings w_1 to w_N:

$$I = w_1 S_1 + w_2 S_2 + \ldots + w_N S_N \tag{8.1}$$

Each of the shares which go to make up the index, S_1 to S_N, has a call option (C_1 to C_N) with respective strike prices ranging from E_1 to E_N. The strike price of the individual index option will simply be equal to the weighted sum of all the individual strike prices:

$$E = w_1 E_1 + w_2 E_2 + \ldots + w_N E_N \tag{8.2}$$

Let's consider the payoff profile at maturity for two portfolios, as outlined in Table 8.1. Portfolio 1 contains an index option, C_I, with strike price X_I.

Portfolio 2 holds options exercisable into each underlying share on the index, with w weights. The index is composed of two shares, S_1 and S_2, with associated call option C_1 and C_2, each with exercise prices E_1 and E_2.

The point is that if both C_1 and C_2 expire in the money or out of the money, the index option will have an identical payoff at maturity. However, if either C_1

Table 8.1: Index options compared to portfolios of individual options

	$S_1 < E_1$ $S_2 < E_2$	$S_1 < E_1$ $S_2 < E_2$	$S_1 < E_1$ $S_2 < E_2$
Portfolio 1			
Long index options C_I	0	$I - E_I$	$\max(0, \ w_1(S_1 - E_1) + w_2(S_2 - E_2))$
Portfolio 2			
Long individual $wC_1 + wC_2$	0	$(wS_1 + wS_2) - w_1(S_1 - E_1)$	
Options on index		$(wE_1 - wE_2)$	
		$= I - E_I$	

or C_2 expire in the money while the other issue expires out of the money, the sum of the individual option profiles is greater than that of the index option, as shown in Table 8.1. Therefore this is an example of *portfolio dominance*, and shows why a portfolio of individual options is never worth less than its index counterpart.

PORTFOLIO SELECTION AND DERIVATIVES

The basic idea of establishing a multivariate hedge is to offset the equity market risk of a given portfolio of derivatives using a composite such as an index future while still being able to benefit from long volatility by dynamically adjusting when the exposure becomes unbalanced.

For those not familiar with the terminology, this is not the same as stock or *cash/index arbitrage*. Cash/index arbitrage is instigated by a group of investors who attempt to 'lock-in' interest rate/dividend benefits when index futures are not trading at 'fair' levels. This will involve buying/selling baskets of shares or 'the cash' versus selling/buying futures when the futures are trading expensive/cheap.

For our multivariate hedger, if there was a warrant/convertible bond on every stock in a given index, it would be possible to buy a delta adjusted amount of each such that a given exposure could be exactly offset using index futures.

We consider a hypothetical example of an index composed of three shares: *A*, *B*, and *C*. Let's assume that an investor could buy \$10 million of exposure in each share, thus giving a total market exposure of \$30 million. Let's now further assume that this hypothetical index has futures outstanding with a contract size equal to \$1 million. In order to neutralise equity market risk, our investor would need to sell 30 contracts.

It should be obvious that if each of the above equities had warrants outstanding (we assume that the convert investor can swap out fixed income), our investor could buy a delta adjusted proportion of warrants to give identical exposure to the underlying.

Let's assume one of the underlying equity components rises substantially so that equity exposure via the derivative rises. We would be required to sell some convertibles/warrants in order to re-establish a market neutral position and effectively 'lock-in' long volatility gains. Of course, another underlying equity component may fall substantially over the same period with consequent reduction in equity exposure via the derivative. This will require us to buy convertibles/warrants in order to re-establish a market neutral position.

In reality, there will only be a limited number of warrants/converts on stocks which we may wish to hedge using futures, but an interesting point has already been raised. Delta adjustments to a multivariate hedge should be made via changes to *long* positions.

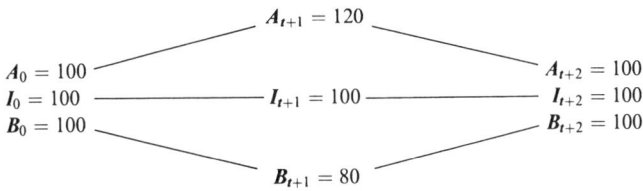

Figure 8.1: Hedge adjustments considered

Figure 8.1 shows the hypothetical path taken by two shares, *A* and *B* and an index, *I*. At the beginning of the period, both *A* and *B* have underlying values equal to 100. The value of the index is also rebased to 100. In time period $t + 1$, the value of *A* rises to 120, *B* falls to 80 and the index remains unchanged at 100. In time period $t + 2$, all values equal 100. $A + B$ track the index throughout the period, but in order to delta adjust, if derivatives were used in lieu of stock, we would have to sell some of *A* converts/warrants in $T + 1$ and buy some of *B* converts/warrants. Furthermore, in $T + 2$ the reverse adjustments would occur and long volatility would ensue.

If total exposure alone was considered, no adjustments and arbitrage profits would have been made. Hedge funds trading baskets are often tempted to adjust using futures because transactions costs are so minimal and the futures are often so liquid. However, by doing so, they are not trading the volatility of the individual shares, which are typically higher than that of the index. In the example considered, we track the index, but there is a desired aspect to the individual shares not being correlated well with each other. In actuality, there may be periods while trading a multivariate hedge, when a given number of positions are due for adjustments because of upside movements in the underlying equity, and, simultaneously, other positions may require adjustments because of downside movements in the underlying equity.

The example of a portfolio of *A*, *B*, and *C* shares above is extremely unrealistic. If we were to think just in terms of buying equity in the S & P 500 or Nikkei 225 at this point, for example, and that we wanted to gain exposure via a subset of stocks, analysts would normally '*beta*' adjust exposure.

Using past observations, beta is a measure of a stock's sensitivity to changes in a given index and is given by the slope of the following equation:

$$r_s = \alpha_{sI} + \beta_{sI} r_I + \epsilon_{sI} \qquad (8.3)$$

where r_s = return on security s
r_I = return on the market
α_{sI} = the intercept, often referred to as 'alpha'
β_{sI} = Beta or slope term
ϵ_{sI} = random error term

This is not the time to rigorously question the validity or usefulness of estimating this statistic. Beta may well be very powerful in terms of describing the characteristics of stocks or groups of stocks under particular conditions, but we just need to consider the implications of using it to adjust portfolio exposure at this point. ϵ is the random error term and is used to show that the 'market' model above does not explain the returns to 's' perfectly.

In our simple example, let's assume that we wish to gain exposure by merely buying stocks A and B rather than buying A, B, and C. Furthermore, the beta of the subset is estimated at 1.1. This means that for a 1% increase/decrease in the market, we would expect our portfolio to increase/decrease 1.1%. It would appear that we would have had to sell 33 contracts then to remain market neutral. This would not make sense for us. Let's see why. If we beta adjust, the level of error introduced could easily completely erase any arbitrage gains from delta adjustments.

Let's assume that the market's return over the period under consideration is 10%. Let's say that we estimate the beta to be 1.1 for security A and therefore sell 10% more exposure in the form of an index future. Our long position in A is held in the form of a warrant with a 50% delta or hedge ratio. By selling 10% more exposure against the position, it is equivalent to increasing the delta.

Now in the example shown in Figure 8.2, the market goes up 10% over the period, but our share only goes up 6% – a random error of 5%. Even a cursory glance at the actual market model lines in Figures 8.3(a)–8.3(d) show this kind of estimation error not to be uncommon at all. Many hedge adjustments would be lost in practice if one was to beta adjust. Moreover, we should not care if individual shares do not track the index well. It is overall market exposure that

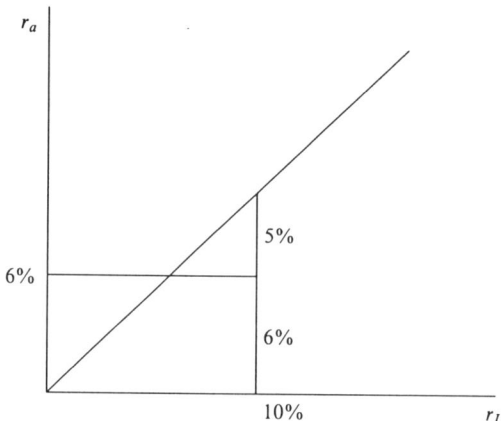

Figure 8.2: Beta of security A

(a)

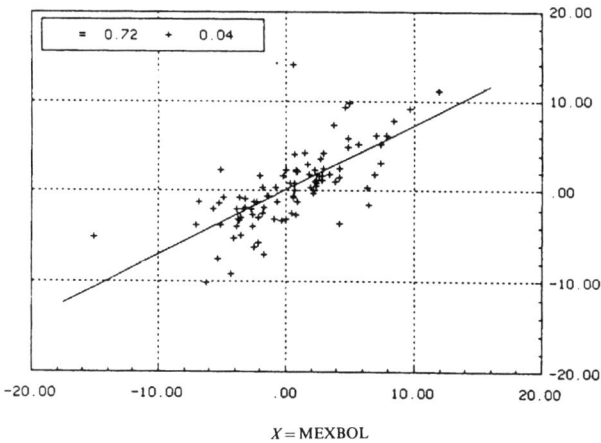

X = MEXBOL

(b)

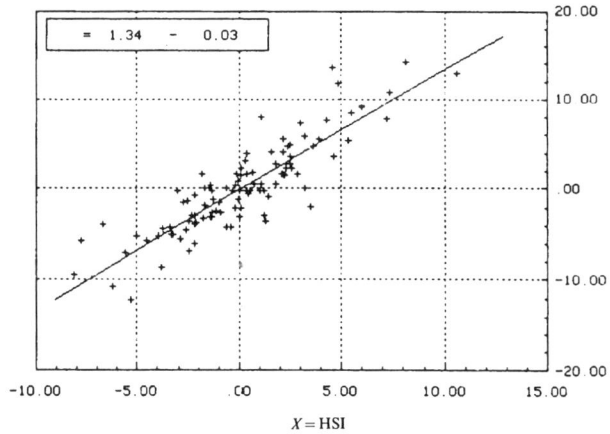

X = HSI

Figure 8.3: Historical beta
Source: Bloomberg, LP.

(c)

PSA PEUGEOT CITROEN

CAC 40 INDEX

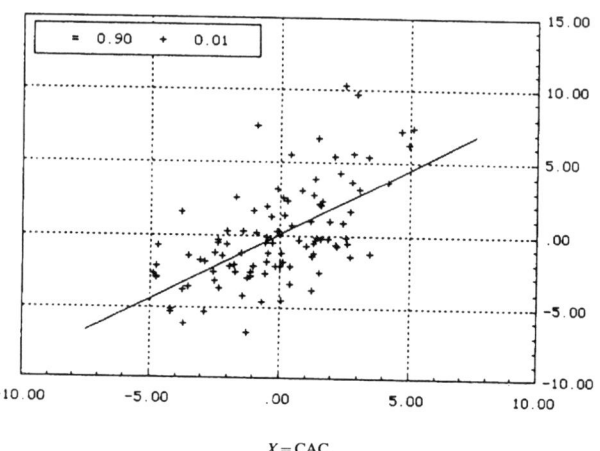

$X = \text{CAC}$

(d)

MICROSOFT CORP

S&P 500 INDEX

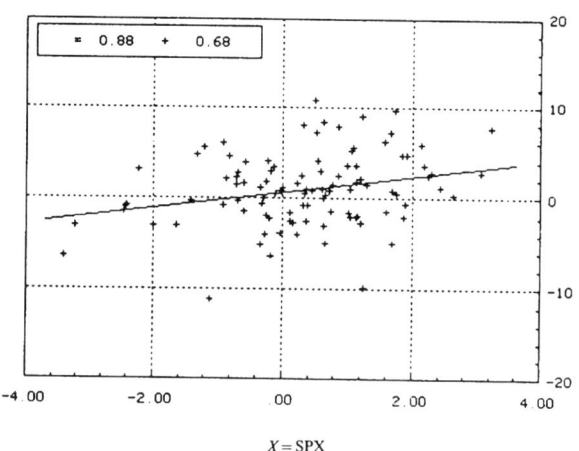

$X = \text{SPX}$

Figure 8.3: (Continued)

is important. In fact, as already shown, lack of correlation between members of the long portfolio is a more profitable characteristic. In practice, then, it is assumed beta is one and tracking is zero. We now consider why.

TRACKING ERROR

The most obvious stumbling block to achieving a multivariate hedge is that of tracking error. *Tracking error* is a measure of the under/outperformance of a given portfolio relative to a given index. If our portfolio increases by 7% in the first quarter of the year relative to an index move of 12% over the same period, then tracking error is equal to −5% or −20% on an annualised basis.

The objective would *appear* to be the minimisation of tracking of our portfolio relative to a given benchmark index while using as few issues as possible. With reference to Figure 8.4(a) let's assume that we wished to track the Nikkei 225. If we were to purchase only one share of the Nikkei 225 stock index, there would be considerable risk of tracking error over the forthcoming period. Conceptually, Figure 8.4(a) illustrates that as we add the second equity, then the third equity and so on, tracking error decreases very quickly to begin with, then tails off until we reach the extreme state where if we were to purchase each and every '225' share, there would be zero tracking error. Those who carry out cash/index arbitrage strategies will be very familiar with this relationship.

It is important for us not to overstate tracking error, however, since we are not merely attempting to minimise tracking error. To see why this is the case, let's consider Figure 8.4(b) which illustrates a *trade-off* between tracking error and the number of cheap issues used in the trade.

Let's think why Figure 8.4(b) looks like this. If one issue alone is hedged against an index, irrespective of how cheap it might be theoretically, there is potential for there to be little correlation between the underlying share and the Nikkei 225 index over the next period. There is a chance that the share may outperform the index by, let's say, 15%, but it might just as easily underperform by 15%. This would be a risky hedge and as can be seen, might actually offer very little hedge potential at all. However, let's think of adding issues to our portfolio, one by one, in order of their having desirable characteristics. To begin with, the issues added will be undervalued theoretically and will simultaneously diversify equity risk, therefore reducing associated tracking error.

However, at some point, the expected return to this strategy will increase at a decreasing rate, and eventually begin to fall. Reasons for this will include the fact that we may be using derivatives which are less and less undervalued, or that in order to reduce tracking error we are forced to use equity or other fairly priced or overvalued securities.

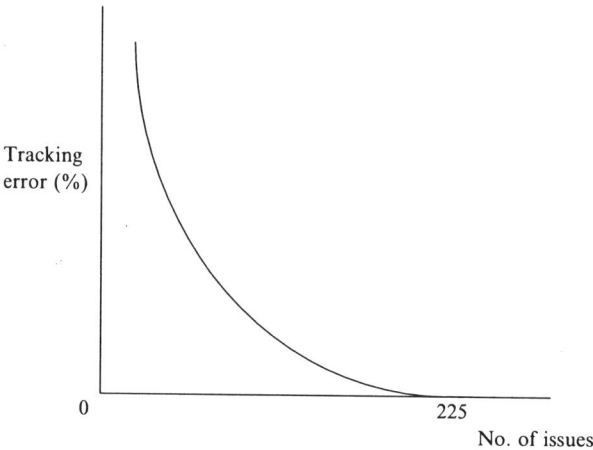

(a) Tracking error versus number of issues

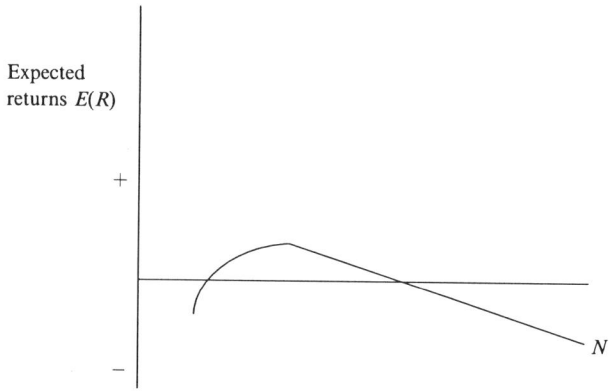

(b) Expected return and the number of issues

Figure 8.4: Tracking error, expected return, and number of issues

A tracking error of ±2% per annum for those carrying out cash/index arbitrage would not be tolerable. However, from our standpoint the option component of our convertible or warrant may be 50% underpriced, for example. It may be optimal to include only thirty-five warrants and convertible bonds versus a futures position with a tracking error of, say, ±3% p.a. since the tracking error risk is offset by the portfolio being 30% underpriced on average. In contrast, in order to bring the tracking error down in any noticeable way, it may be the case that any opportunity to make an arbitrage gain is completely lost by the portfolio not being undervalued enough.

Figure 8.5 illustrates the actual performance of a basket hedge strategy run over the period February 1991 through to June 1992, by *Cresvale* International Asset Management in Japan against the Nikkei 225 Index futures. The performance shown is an *unleveraged* one, but is useful for a number of reasons.

Typically, 30–40 issues were included in the long portfolio at any one time. However, because issues are sometimes removed and replaced when they become expensive, the effect is that from a tracking error perspective, it feels as if there are more issues in the basket. A market neutral stance was taken at all times and any imbalance caused by substantial share price advances or declines was neutralised via adjustments to the long positions. As with all hedging, 'bumpiness' of the return profile resulted from a number of factors.

The 'carry' on these trades is an important characteristic. Index futures will reflect relevant prevailing interest rates. At the beginning of the period under consideration, the 'stand-still' return to the trade was in excess of 10%. At the same time, when marking to market, the futures will be written in sometimes at substantial discounts or premiums to 'fair' value. Most noticeable is the fact that long positions in the derivatives become cheaper and more expensive at times and although this issue was addressed in Chapter 7, it is interesting to note extreme conditions.

The long volatility nature of the trade is very apparent, with the basket making advances in falling, rising, and sideways markets. It is particularly during non-volatile periods that the 'carry' considerations, already mentioned , become crucial.

The same strategy outlined has been used not from a hedge standpoint but also by those who wish to effectively enhance exposure to a given equity benchmark composite or index, by *synthesising equity*. The benchmark might actually have no future on it at all, such as an over the counter market (OTC). Using a basket approach with derivatives in such circumstances is also likely to greatly enhance liquidity.

ADVANTAGES AND DISADVANTAGES OF MULTIVARIATE PERSPECTIVE

Multivariate hedging has both advantages and disadvantages. Only a limited number of funds use this kind of trading, although those that do tend to be large participants. The main reason for this is that many funds do not wish to assume additional risks associated with this kind of strategy, particularly those relating to tracking error. Moreover, many markets simply do not have enough cheap corporate derivatives to merit establishing the trade against futures.

Prime brokers are, on the whole, less familiar with basket type hedging. Leverage on baskets is gradually becoming more competitive but it still does

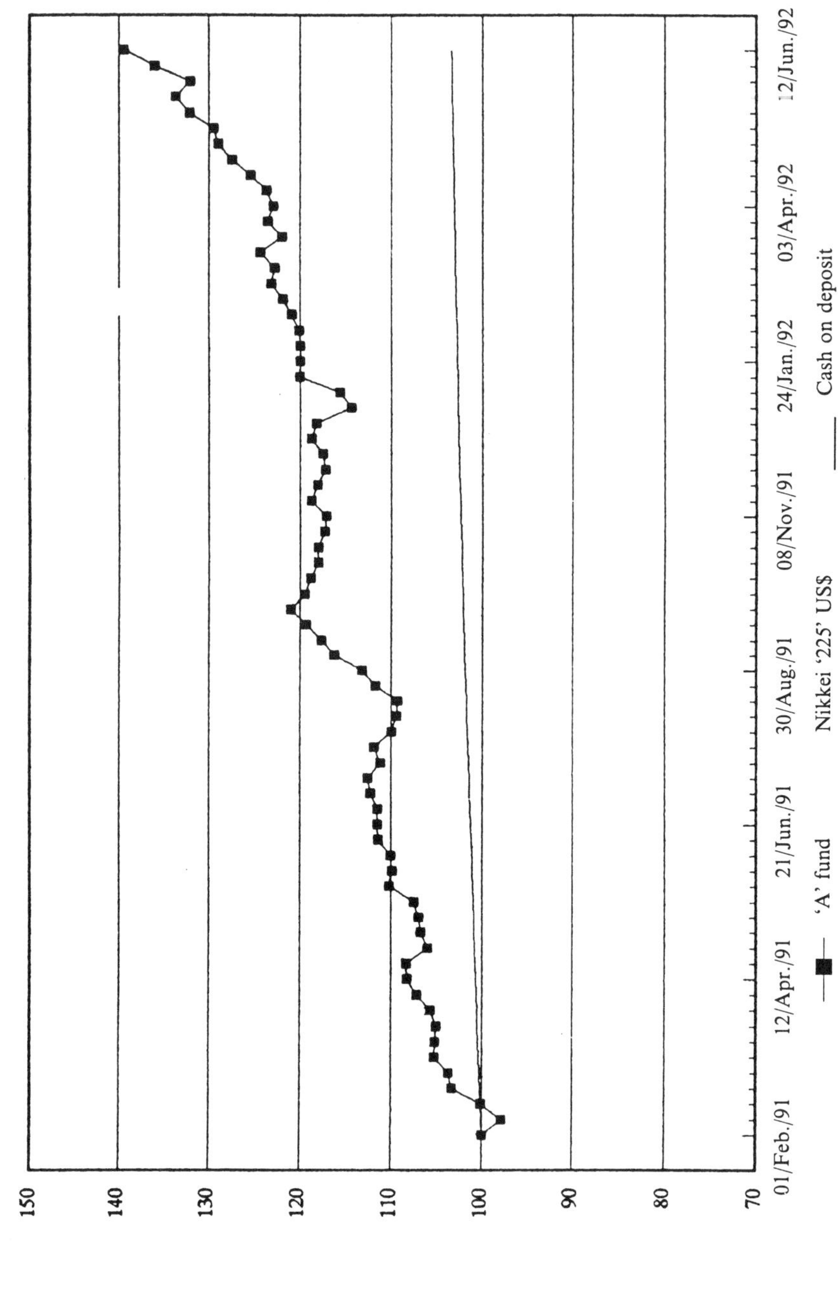

Figure 8.5: Basket hedge strategy: Cresvale 'A' Fund Ltd, February 1991–June 1992

not provide anywhere near the leverage that may be achieved on particular hedge positions against individual shares. This ties in with the important issue of default risk. As discussed in earlier chapters, a hedger of converts is subject to the disadvantages of a defaulting bond to the extent that he is unhedged. If hedged against futures, the convert holder is exposed. For this reason, the hedger would have to 'swap' out the fixed income component of the convert, so that in effect he was trading a warrant basket.

Basket type trading definitely enhances *flexibility and liquidity* to market places. From a hedge standpoint, first, borrowing stock is no longer relevant. With regard to corporate derivatives, it is a fact that if it is not possible to borrow the share, then it would not be unusual for the derivative to trade at a discount to its fair value, irrespective of the fact that shareholders could replace their existing holdings with alternative exposure. By using futures it would therefore be possible to hedge issues where the equity cannot be sold short. Alternatively, it may be the case that it is possible to borrow good size in a share but that the liquidity in the underlying equity is so thin that it would not be practical to build a decent position in the hedge. Another aspect is that there are periods of temporary disequilibrium in stock loan, when for example blocks of shares may be '*recalled*'. Such circumstances can prove particularly disadvantageous to hedge funds who may be left exposed to market risks. Hedge fund managers are typically happier to sell futures to hedge out this kind of problem if they feel that the underlying share has underperformed the index.

Bibliography

Acharya, S. and Handa, P. (1988) 'Early calls of convertible debt: new evidence and theory', New York University, Saloman Brothers Center for the Study of Financial Institutions, *Working Paper* (June).

Aldred, P. (1987) 'Convertibles and warrants', London: Euromoney Publications.

Armstrong, H.T. (1954) 'Stock option warrants – caveats for the speculator', *The Analysts Journal* (May).

Bachelier, L. (1900) 'Theorie de la spéculation', reprinted in Paul H. Cootner (ed.), *The Random Character of Stock Market Prices* (Cambridge, MA: MIT Press, 1967) 17–78.

Bierman, H. (1973) 'The cost of warrants', *Journal of Financial and Quantitative Analysis* (June), 499–503.

Bird, A.P. (1971) 'Evaluating warrants', *The Investment Analyst* (December).

Black, F. (1975) 'Fact and fantasy in the use of options', *Financial Analysts Journal*, 31 (July–August), 36–41; 61–72.

———(1976) 'The pricing of commodity contracts', *Journal of Financial Economics*, 3, 167–79.

Black, F. and Cox, J. (1976) 'Valuing corporate securities: some effects of bond indenture provisions', *Journal of Finance*, 31 (May), 351–68.

Black, F. and Scholes, M. (1972) 'The valuation of option contracts and a test of market efficiency', *Journal of Finance*, 27 (May), 399–418.

———(1973) 'The pricing of options and corporate liabilities', *Journal of Political Economy*, 81, 637–59.

Black, F., Dermam, E. and Toy, W. (1990) 'A one-factor model of interest rates and its application to Treasury Bond options', *Financial Analysts Journal*, 46 (January–February).

Brennan, M. and Schwartz, E. (1977) 'Convertible bonds: valuation and optimal strategies for call and conversion', *Journal of Finance*, 32 (December), 1699–1715.

———(1980) 'Analysing convertible bonds', *Journal of Financial and Quantitative Analysis*, 15 (November), 907–29.

———(1986) 'The case for convertibles', *Chase Financial Quarterly*, 1, 27–46.

Calamos, J.P. (1988) *Investing in Convertible Securities* (London: Longman).

Castanias, R., Chung, K. and Johnson, H. (1988) 'Dividend spreads', *Journal of Business*, 61, 299–313.

Chen, A.H.Y. (1970) 'A model of warrant pricing in a dynamic market', *Journal of Finance*, 25 (December), 1041–60.

Connolly, K.B. and Philips, G.A. (1992) *Japanese Warrant Markets* (London: Macmillan).

Constantinides, G. and Grundy, B. (1987) 'Call and conversion of convertible corporate bonds: theory and evidence', University of Chicago, *Working Paper* (January).

Constantinides, G., and Rosenthal, R.W. (1984) 'Strategic analysis of the competitive exercise of certain financial options', *Journal of Economic Theory*, 32 (February).

Cooper, I. (1988) 'The relationship between two methods of valuing convertible bonds', London Business School.

Courtadon, G. and Merrick, J., Jr. (1983) 'The option pricing model and the valuation of corporate securities', *Midland Corporate Finance Journal*, 1 (Autumn), 43–57.

Cowan, A.R., Nandkumar, N. and Singh, A.K. (1990) 'Stock returns before and after calls of convertible bonds', *Journal of Financial and Quantitative Analysis*, 25, 549–54.

———— (1993) 'Calls and out of the money convertible bonds', *Financial Management*, 22, 105–16.

Cox, J., Ross, S. and Rubinstein, M. (1979) 'Option pricing: a simplified approach', *Journal of Financial Economics*, 7(3) (September), 229–63.

———— (1985) *Options Markets* (Englewood Cliffs, NJ: Prentice-Hall).

Cretien, P.D. Jr., (1969) 'Convertible bond premiums as predictors of common stock price changes', *Financial Analysts Journal* (November–December), 90–5.

———— (1970) 'Convertible premiums vs. stock prices', *Financial Analysts Journal*, 25, 917–22.

Crouhy, M. and Galai, D. (1988) 'Warrant valuation and equity volatility', *HEC*, Paris.

Curry, D.W. (1971) 'A comprehensive financial reporting method for convertible debt', *The Accounting Review*, 45, 490–503.

Dann, L.Y. and Mikkelson W.H. (1984) 'Convertible debt issuance, capital structure change and financing related information: some new evidence', *Journal of Financial Economics*, 13, 157–86.

Davidson, W.N. III, Glascock, J.L. and Won Jon Koh (1993) 'A test of the tax-induced leveraged hypothesis in convertible securities: a note', *Journal of Business, Finance and Accounting*, 20, 99–106.

Dawson, S.M. (1974) 'Timing interest payments for convertible bonds, *Financial Management*, 3, 14–18.

DeBerg, C.L. (1990) 'Earnings per share and actual conversion of convertible securities', *Journal of Accounting Education*, 8, 137–51.

Douglas, L.G. (1990) *Bond Risk Analysis* (New York: New York Institute of Finance).

Dudley, L.W. and Schadler, F.P. (1994) 'Reporting the relative equity portion of convertible debt issues', *Journal of Accounting, Auditing and Financing*, 23, 273–302.

Dunn, K. and Eades, K. (1989) 'Voluntary conversion of convertible securities and the options call strategy', *Journal of Financial Economics*, 23, 273–301.

Duvell, D.T. (1970) 'Premiums on convertible bonds: comment', *Journal of Finance*, 25, 923–7.

Emery, D.R., Iskander-Datta, M.E. and Jong-Chul Rhim (1994) 'Capital structure management as a motivation for calling convertible debt', *Journal of Financial Research*, 17, 91–104.

Emmanuel, D. (1983a) 'Warrant valuation and exercise strategy', *Journal of Financial Economics*, 12 (August), 211–36.

————(1983b) 'A theoretical model for valuing preferred stock', *Journal of Finance*, 38 (September), 1133–55.

Fernandez, P.A. (1993) 'An analysis of Spanish convertible bonds', *Advances in Options and Futures Research*, 5, 367–92.

Fields, L.P. and Mais, E.L. (1991) 'The valuation effects of private placements of convertible debt', *Journal of Finance*, 46, 1925–32.

Figlewski, S. Silber, W.L. and Subrahmanyam, M.G. (1990) 'Financial options: from theory to practice', *Stern*, New York University.

Frank, W.G. and Kroncke, C.O. (1974) 'Classifying conversions of convertible debentures over four years', *Financial Management*, 3, 33–9.

Frank, W.G. and Weygandt, J.J. (1970) 'Convertible debt and earnings per share: Pragmatism vs. good theory', *The Accounting Review*, 45, 280–9.

Fried, S. (1971) *Speculating with Warrants* (New York: RHM Associates).

Galai, D. and Masulis, R.W. (1976) 'The option pricing model and the risk factor of stock', *Journal of Financial Economics*, 3 (January–March).

Galai, D. and Schneller, M. (1978) 'Pricing warrants and the value of the firm', *Journal of Finance*, 33 (December), 1333–42.

Gastineau, G. (1988) *The Options Manual* (New York: McGraw-Hill).

Gaumnitz, B.R. and Thomson, J.E. (1987) 'Establishing the common stock equivalence of convertible bonds', *The Accounting Review*, 62, 601–22.

Gemmill, G. (1993) *Options Pricing* (New York: McGraw Hill International).

Geske, R. (1977) 'The valuation of corporate liabilities as compound options', *Journal of Financial and Quantitative Analysis*, 12 (November), 541–52.

Giguere, G. (1958) 'Warrants: a mathematical model of evaluation', *Analysts Journal* (14 November).

Green, R.C. (1984) 'Investment incentives, debt, and warrants', *Journal of Financial Economics*, 13, 115–36.

Hallis, J.S. (1976) 'Should companies issue warrants?', unpublished thesis, MIT (May).

Harris, M. and Raviv, A. (1985) 'A sequential signalling model of convertible debt call policy', *Journal of Finance*, 40, 1263–81.

Hilliard, E.J. and Leitch, R.A. (1977) 'Analysis of the warrant hedge in a stable paretian market', *Journal of Financial and Quantitative Analysis* (March), 85–99.

Ho, T.S.Y. and Lee, S.B. (1986) 'Term structure movements and pricing interest rate contingent claims', *Journal of Finance* (December), 1–22.

Ho, T.S.Y. and Singer, R. (1982) 'Bond indenture provisions and the risk of corporate debt', *Journal of Financial Economics*, 10 (December), 375–406.

Hsia, C-C. (1981) 'Optimal debt of a firm: an option pricing approach', *Journal of Financial Research*, 4 (Autumn), 221–31.

Hubbard, C.L. and Johnson, T. (1969) 'Writing calls with convertible bonds', 25, 78–89.

Hull, J. (1989) *Options, Futures and Other Derivative Securities* (Englewood Cliffs, NJ: Prentice-Hall).

Ingersoll, J., Jr. (1977) 'An examination of convertible call policies on convertible securities', *Journal of Finance*, 32 (May), 463–78.

————(1977) 'A contingent-claims valuation of convertible securities', *Journal of Financial Economics*, 4 (May), 289–322.

Jennings, E.H. (1974) 'An estimate of convertible bond premiums', *Journal of Financial and Quantitative Analysis*, 1, 33–56.

————(1975) 'Reply: An estimate of convertible bond premiums', *Journal of Financial and Quantitative Analysis*, 2, 375–6.

Jennergren, P. and Sorensson, T. (1991) 'On the choice of model in convertible valuation – a case study', *Omega*, 19, 185–96.

Kassouf, S.T. (1969a) *Evaluation of Convertible Securities* (New York: Analytic Publishers).

——(1969b) 'An econometric model for option price with implications for investors' expectations and audacity', *Econometrica*, 17, 685–94.

Kim Yong-Cheol and Stulz, R.M. (1992) 'Is there a global market for convertible bonds', *Journal of Business*, 65, 75–92.

King, R.D. (1984) 'The effect of convertible bond equity values on dilution and leverage', *The Accounting Review*, 59, 419–31.

————(1986) 'Convertible bond valuation: an empirical test', *Journal of Financial Research*, 9, 53–69.

Latane, H.A. and Rendleman, R.J., Jr. (1976) 'Standard deviations of stock price ratios implied in option prices', *Journal of Finance*, 31 (May), 369–82.

Lauterbach, B. and Schultz, P. (1990) 'Pricing warrants: an empirical study of the Black–Scholes model and its alternatives', *Journal of Finance*, 45(4), 1181–1209.

Leabo, D.A. and Rogalski, R. (1975) 'Warrant price movements and the efficient market model', *Journal of Finance*, 30 (March), 163–177.

Lee, C.J. (1981) 'The pricing of corporate debt: a note', *Journal of Finance*, 36 (December), 1187–9.

Leibowitz, M.L. (1974) 'Understanding convertible securities', *Financial Analysts Journal*, 30, 57–67.

Lewis, C.M. (1991) 'Convertible debt: valuation and conversion in complex capital structures', *Journal of Banking and Finance*, 15, 665–82.

Lin, J.C. and Chen, K.C. (1991) 'Partially anticipated convertible calls', *Financial Review*, 26, 501–16.

Marshall, J.F. and Kapner, K.R. (1993a) *Understanding Swaps* (London: John Wiley).

————(1993b) *The Swaps Market* (London: Kolb Publishing).

Mason, S.P. and Bhattacharya, S. (1981) 'Risky debt, jump processes, and safety covenants', *Journal of Financial Economics*, 9 (September), 281–307.

McMillan, L. (1986) *Options as a Strategic Investment* (New York: New York Institute of Finance).

McGuire, S. (1990) *Convertibles* (Cambridge: Woodhead-Faulkner).

Merton, R.C. (1975) 'On corporate debt: the risk structure of interest rates', *Journal of Finance*, 29 (March), 449–70.

————(1973) 'Theory of rational option pricing', *Bell Journal of Economics and Management Science*, 4 (Spring), 141–83.

Mikkelson, W.H. (1981) 'Convertible calls and security returns', *Journal of Financial Economics*, 9, 237–64.

————(1983) 'Capital structure change and decreases in stockholders' wealth: a cross-sectional study of convertible security calls', National Bureau of Economics Research, Working Paper, 1137.

Modigliani, F. and Miller, M. (1958) 'The cost of capital, corporation finance and the theory of investment', *American Economic Review*, 48 (June), 261–97.

Noreen, E. and Wolfson, M. (1981) 'Equilibrium warrant pricing models and accounting for executive stock options', *Journal of Accounting Research*, 19 (Autumn), 384–98.

Ofer, A.R. and Natarajan, A. (1987) 'Convertible call policies: an empirical analysis of an information-signalling hypothesis', *Journal of Financial Economics* 19, 91–108.

Parkinson, M. (1977) 'Option pricing: the American put', *Journal of Business*, 50 (January).

Philips, G.A. (1988) *Japanese Warrant Markets* (London: IFR Publishing).

Rush, D.F. and Melicher, R.W. (1974) 'An empirical examination of factors which influence warrant prices', *Journal of Finance*, 29 (December), 1449–66.

Schulz, G. and Trautman, S. (1990) 'Valuation of warrants: theory and empirical tests for warrants written on German stocks', University of Stuttgart.

Schwartz, E.S. (1977) 'The valuation of warrants: implementing a new approach', *Journal of Financial Economics*, 4 (January), 79–93.

Shelton, J.P. (1967) 'The relation of the pricing of a warrant to the price of its associated common stock', *Financial Analysts Journal*, 23 (May–June and July–August), 88–99.

Singh, A.K. and Arnold, R.C. (1991) 'Underwritten calls of convertible bonds', *Journal of Financial Economics*, 29, 173–95.

Smith, C. (1976) 'Option pricing: a review', *Journal of Financial Economics*, 3 (January–March), 3–51.

Spatt, C. and Sterbenz, F. (1988) 'Warrant exercise, dividends and reinvestment policy', *Journal of Finance*, 43, 493–506.

Stigum, M. (1981) *Money Market Calculations: Yields, Break-Evens, and Arbitrage* (Homewood, IL.: Dow Jones–Irwin).

Thorp., E.O. and Kassouf, S.T. (1967) *Beat the Market: A Scientific Stock Market System* (New York: Random House).

Vasicek, O.A. (1977) 'An equilibrium characterisation of the term structure', *Journal of Financial Economics*, 5 (November), 177–88.

Walter, J.E. and Que, A.V (1973) 'The valuation of convertible bonds', *Journal of Finance*, 28, 713–32.

Index

warrant investors   14, 15
warrants   15, 30, 59, 100–1
  cum warrants   12, 34, 35
Wharf Holdings   127

yield   3, 65, 87–8
  credit rating and   88, 89
  current   11
  price/yield curves
    see price/yield curves

yield advantage   11
  see also payoff analysis
yield curves   60–6, 115, 117
'yield to put'   51

zero coupon convertible bonds   32–5, 65